Ivan Mauger's World Speedway Book

Ove Fundin and Ivan Mauger. Between them, they hold twenty World titles

Ivan Mauger's World Speedway Book

Edited by

IVAN MAUGER & PETER OAKES

PELHAM BOOKS

First published in Great Britain by
PELHAM BOOKS LTD
52 Bedford Square
London, WC1B 3EF
1973

ISBN 0 7207 0725 0

Printed in Great Britain by Hollen Street Press Ltd
at Slough and bound by Dorstel Press at Harlow.

Contents

Acknowledgements

The authors' thanks are due to all those who have helped in the compilation of this book, and in particular the photographers whose pictures have been reproduced as illustrations: Des C. & R. J. Lawrence, Michael Patrick, Dennis Greene, BBC TV, *Daily Express*, S.K.R. Photo International, Dick Barrie, Wright Wood, M. Carling, Derrick Penman, Industrial Pictorial Services, Johannes Wanke, *Sunday Times* (Perth, Australia), V. C. Browne, Edward Sokoloroski, Ralph W. Currier, A. C. Weedon, Lars Edgren Pressbild.

Igor Plechanov—five times Russian champion

Foreword

Nineteen-seventy-three marked speedway's coming-of-age.

Not in a numerical sense, since the sport has been with us for far longer than the golden 21 years.

But in every other sense of the word as the sport received its biggest-ever publicity boost with half a dozen or more big newspapers jumping on to the speedway band-wagon.

Television, too, began to notice speedway with London Weekend Television devoting more time to televising the shale game than any other motorised sport.

And so did the big-time sponsors who have finally come round to realising the vast potential in a sport that attracts more people through its turnstiles than any other sport except soccer.

Ivan Mauger is one of the people who has helped give speedway its big push-forward. He's one of the country's jet-set sportsmen and his continued high placings in the *Daily Express* and BBC Sports Personality of the Year pools illustrates not only his immense popularity—but the popularity of a sport that looked like dying in the late fifties.

Throughout the sixties it was given a slow kiss of life until now—the seventies —it has embarked on a golden era.

Domestic success has given birth to international success and this summer saw the launching of the first genuine World League with riders from the four corners of the globe flocking to Britain for a three-week fiesta of action.

The international appeal of the sport is, we hope, reflected in this book.

Top names in world journalism—names like Peter White, Alan Clark and Ian MacDonald—have joined together with some of Britain's most eminent speedway figures to make this not only an entertaining but an authoritative book, and to reflect speedway's growing emergence as an off-shoot of show business as well as sport, the BBC's radio personality David Hamilton has penned his own views of a sport in which he is actively engaged.

Many of speedway's top photographers have caught some of the infinite spectacle of the sport through the lens, and between these covers you should find much about world speedway that has hitherto remained the secret domaine of those living in Australia. New Zealand, Poland, Russia, Germany or Sweden.

Britain has moved into Europe in recent years—we trust that this book, the first to cover the global influence of speedway, will help to break down any barriers that may exist between countries.

Whether you support Exeter or Leningrad; whether you watch your speedway at Melbourne or Wroclaw, we hope there is something for you in the pages that follow.

SPEEDWAY'S GOLDEN BOY

Ivan Mauger on the Golden Bike, with George Wenn (left) and Ray Bokelman

They call him the Golden Boy of World Speedway.

And it isn't purely Ivan Mauger's on-track exploits that have earned him that tag.

Because he's got something to prove he really is the sport's golden boy ... a £9,000 gold-plated Jawa machine and a £1,000 gold-plated safety helmet to go with it.

Everyone in speedway knows by now that the bike was presented to Ivan by two American enthusiasts after they'd promised to gold-plate his machine if he won three world finals in a row. But what is not known is how he came to meet them—and how they came to make a promise that ended up with him owning probably the world's most expensive motor cycle.

Ivan first went to America in October 1968 to ride in three meetings at the now-closed Whiteman Stadium in Paicomo, California, a few miles outside Los Angeles.

All the preliminary negotiations had been done through Harry Oxley, who was manager of a motor cycle shop owned by former World Speedway champion Jack Milne in Pasadena. Unhappily there were a few problems surrounding the promotion because the track was not governed by the international-controllng

FIM and because of this the promoter pulled out with only a week or so to go before the scheduled meeting. Rather than cancel the meetings Harry Oxley and Jack Milne took over as promoters and within a few days had sorted out the situation with the FIM.

It was at the first meeting at Whiteman that Ivan was introduced to an ex-patriate Englishman—George Wenn.

George had been a speedway enthusiast when he was living in England and at one time had been mechanic to the Norwich National League side. He'd also looked after Alf Hagon's machines when the British drag champion was a star performer on Britain's grass-tracks.

It was this experience that had made George a valuable member of the

Ivan Mauger and the £9,000 gold-plated Jawa at the 1972 Motor Cycle Show at London's Earls Court

Toasting the Golden Boy—American promoter Harry Oxley (left) and Charles Tinch, president of Premier Pacific Helmets Inc who presented Ivan with a £1,000 gold-plated helmet to mark his double World Championship success in 1972

Californian speedway set-up and he was put in charge of a neat-looking Jap machine owned by Californian businessman Ray Bokelman's wife Ethel.

Under the American system as it operated, most machines were owned by sponsors and they would also provide a tuner who would keep the bike in prime condition. All the rider was expected to do was turn up for the meeting, ride the machine and hand over a percentage of his prize money to the sponsor.

George and Ivan became friends very quickly and it was George and his wife Freda who showed Ivan some of the sights of California, including his first ever visit to Disneyland.

A year later Ivan returned for another season in the States and stayed with the Wenns, something he and his wife Raye have done every time they've gone to America.

It wasn't until the second trip that Ivan met Ray Bokelman, a close friend of the Wenns. For the trip Ivan took over the Jawa on which he'd won his second world championship at Wembley, although he never rode it in the States as George had already arranged a machine to be available for him.

At that time Ivan had no idea that Ray Bokelman was recognised as one of the leading metal-platers in the States—a recognition that brought him many government contracts.

Says Ivan: 'Several times Ray looked at my Wembley bike in George's garage and I remember thinking that he wasn't very impressed with it.

'Usually I pride myself on having the smartest bikes in speedway but after

13

an English season the bike does look a little bit tatty no matter how hard one tries to keep it neat.

'I intended leaving the bike with George while I returned to England and to pick it up on the way to Australia and New Zealand.

'George kept dropping a few hints that it looked too rough a machine to be owned by a double World Champion and a couple of days before my American trip was to end he and Ray asked me if I would like them to tidy it up a bit before I came through in January.

'I left it at that—expecting to find the bike a bit cleaner in January and thinking that perhaps they'd polish up a few of the rough spots.'

They went much further than that. When Ivan arrived in Los Angeles en route to Chrischurch he could hardly believe it.

'I'd never seen a bike like it,' he said. 'George had completely stripped every part of the bike including the wheels and engine. Even small details like the carburetter and magneto had been stripped and chromed.

'Ray had plated most of the bike and blue anadized the other parts to blend in.

'It looked so good that I didn't want to ride it and I almost decided that I'd arrange to fly one of my other bikes from England so that I would have another machine to race in Australia.

'It was when I told George and Ray that I couldn't possibly ride the chromed bike that they made their golden promise.

'They told me: "Ride this one and if you win the world final again this year we'll gold-plate the bike for you." At that time I was trying *not* to think of the following year's World Final.

'However I decided I would use the chromed machine for all my meetings in Australia and New Zealand and it caused a sensation at every track at which I appeared.

'As far as I was concerned I'd forgotten about the golden promise and nothing more was said through the 1970 season.

'I didn't give it a second thought until after I'd won the World Final in Wroclaw, Poland, in September that year.

'In the few days after the final I was too interested in other things to remember a promise made some months earlier but a week or so after the Polish trip I received an air mail letter from the States.

'Briefly it said "what's happend to that bike—we are waiting to get started on it." Naturally I wasted no time in taking the bike out to Manchester's Ringway

World Speedway Champion Ivan Mauger, made a guest appearance on Blue Peter when he told Peter Purves and the viewers about his magnificent gold-plated bike, and also showed his world Speedway Championship trophy

Airport and it was on the plane to Los Angeles within a few days.

'Even then I didn't really believe they would do what they had promised.'

Fourteen months later Ivan knew the promise had come good.

Amidst a battery of television and newspaper cameras he was presented with the gold-plated Jawa at a ceremony arranged by George Wenn and Ray Bokelman.

It was George who had stripped the bike down and Ray who had gold-plated the parts before George rebuilt it all.

The bike captured the headlines in the States and took 'Best Bike of the Show' at the famous Long Beach Motor-Cycle show. The American union of metal-platers were so impressed with Ray's work that they built a recruiting film around the gold bike as an example of what can be achieved by a skilled metal-plater.

Said Ivan: 'I couldn't speak when I first saw the bike. It was incredible. Even now I have to gasp every now and again when I look at the incredible workmanship that has gone into it.

Now there's a golden helmet to go with the golden bike. At the party thrown to hand over the bike was Chuck Tinch, president of the American motor-cycle helmet company Premier Pacific Incorporated who had agreed a big sponsorship deal with Ivan for the 1972 season.

At the end of the year the company celebrated Ivan's speedway and long track world championship success by presenting him with the £1,000 gold-plated helmet.

15

And the Golden Boy of Speedway was able to enjoy the golden moments —especially when he became . . .

THE FLYING FALCON

At the beginning of the 1973 season Ivan Mauger joined Exeter for a record signing-on fee—and a contract that included a clause that a private plane would be placed at his disposal for all home meetings and his frequent trips to the Continent. He quickly became part of the Exeter set-up; and here is seen with new team-mates Scott Autrey (left) and Kevin Holden.

He also linked up with Cornishman Chris Julian, Bob Kilby—later to join Oxford in an exchange deal that took Tony Lomas to Exeter—New Zealander Frank Shuter and local boy Bob Coles.

Chris Julian   *Bob Coles*

16

A Chink of Light
by Peter White

On the tarmac at Kawaguchi Speedway, Tokio

Japan will never produce a World Speedway Champion.

Nor will she enter the arena of Test matches and internationals against other speedway nations of the world.

Sweeping statements perhaps . . . but true . . . unless the government of the country has a dramatic change of heart.

For speedway in this mysterious oriental land is so divorced from the accepted version of the sport elsewhere around the globe that Japan exists in a totally isolated cocoon.

A cocoon shrouded in an aura of mysticism.

Almost every aspect of 'speedway' in Japan—and that's exactly what the Easterners call their brand of racing—is different to that known anywhere else in the world.

And it all boils down to the government of the land.

For the government of Japan completely controls speedway racing.

This is a direct result of one of the most unusual, yet most prominent, features of speedway in the Land of the Rising Sun—GAMBLING. And, as a result of government intervention, comes another unique feature—ASPHALT TRACKS. It is because all her speedway tracks are asphalted that Japan is so restricted in making progress on the world scene.

The riders have acquired a completely different style to that required for dirt tracking and can hardly be expected to switch overnight. Thus they are automatically ruled out of such competitions as the World Championship and Test matches.

Unfortunately it's none of the riders' own doing.

There was a time when they conformed with the rest of the world and Japan had every chance of emerging into a speedway power just as the East Europeans have done over the past fifteen or so years.

Speedway began in this obscure, yet so motorcycle-conscious land, around 1950. In those days four *dirt* tracks were in operation. As the sport progressed, several competitors ventured forth to broaden their experience overseas.

Australia and New Zealand were treated to the talents of solo motorcycle riders, Junichi 'Jimmy' Ogisu and Nanae Akomoto—possibly the world's last remaining woman speedway rider who sadly is now blind and unable to race— and midget speedcar driver, Hideyuki 'Happy' Hirano, in the early 1960s. All performed well but then disappeared back to Japan and obscurity.

Until nearly a decade later . . . when Ogisu made another appearance on the world scene. This time he began his tour Down Under and widened his horizons by journeying to Britain.

His appearance in the 1970 Internationale at Wimbledon was the first by a Japanese rider in European speedway.

But, although immensely popular with his endearing manner and quaint ways, it was readily evident wherever Ogisu rode that the gap between Japanese speedway and the rest of the world had widened drastically—thanks to a bill passed by the government in 1968 to asphalt *all* Japanese speedway tracks.

This, strangely, was done in the interests of safety!

The government considered *dirt tracks too dangerous*!

Quite a few of the old hands took time to adapt to the asphalt and even now the likes of Ogisu and present Japanese Champion, Takeo Sato, who is now in his late thirties and at the veteran stage, would much prefer to return to the dirt.

In fact Ogisu has retired because of the dangers associated with the asphalt tracks and Sato hankers after an overseas trip to any country, simply to renew his experience with pukka dirt tracking.

The new breed of Japanese riders, however, are being groomed totally on asphalt tracks and their chances of making the shift to dirt during their careers are almost negligible.

Asphalt speedway is exciting in its own way. Spills are fewer and in all fairness, during a full Sunday afternoon meeting at the Kawaguchis peedway,

(Above) Riders are addressed by the Police Inspector before a meeting, while *(below)* pushers line up the bikes ready for the start

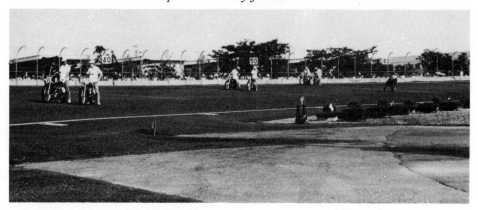

near Tokyo, I did not witness one fall in the ten races staged.

But I dread to think of the consequences should the leading rider tumble, with up to seven other bikes right on his rear wheel!

Most of the excitement for the Japanese spectators, however, lies in the *gambling*. It is gambling that is the life-blood of the game in Japan. This aspect lures crowds of between 20,000 and 30,000 to meetings in the Tokyo area.

And with the gambling come several other completely unique features— like riders being gaoled for allegedly 'fixing' races . . . disqualified for life for jumping the start . . . and locked-up overnight during two-day meetings so they have no contact with outsiders.

Stringent security prevails.

The pit area is built in such a way that competitors are completely segregated from the spectators and it is virtually impossible to liaise in any way.

There are no telephone facilities in the pits and riders are driven in a truck to the starting line about 20 minutes before the commencement of each race. There they are locked in a small room which only the Inspector of Police may enter. Their bikes are wheeled to a shelter on the infield by special track staff.

At the sound of a siren, the riders assemble near the starting line and are addressed by the Police Inspector. He repeats instructions, asks them if they are ready to race and wishes them a safe journey. The riders reply, bow and proceed on several practice laps. Throughout the meeting observers are situated in high towers on each of the four corners.

Generally there are eight riders per race, on a handicap basis, from a clutch start. The riders are all professionals and most are in their late twenties or early thirties. To gain a start on a programme a novice must attend a training school for *six months*. He is then graded according to his times in special testing sessions.

Riders before a race in Japan are locked away in security rooms!

Japanese speedway champion Takeo Sato

There are presently about 400 riders in Japanese speedway and competition is fierce, because, for the top boys it can be a highly profitable occupation. Preliminary events carry about 50,000 yen for a win (about £90) and main events pay about 70,000 yen for a win (about £125).

Riders must provide and maintain their own machines—a costly matter in Japan—but the government supplies all other racing equipment such as helmets, masks, gloves, knee and shoulder pads, etc.

Machines are not, rather paradoxically for such a well known motorcycle manufacturing nation, the renowned Suzukis, Yamahas, etc. but instead little-known Meguros (500 cc), Kyokutos (500 cc), and Triumphs (650 cc) and Nortons (750 cc). The former two engines are manufactured exclusively in Japan.

The engine capacity in Japanese speedway is 1500 cc and all units run on petrol as opposed to alcohol elsewhere in the world.

Japan's own speedway engine—the 500 c.c. Kyokuto fitted with Dellorto carburettor in a standard Jawa frame

The style of a Japanese rider

Some Hondas have been tried, but with only limited success. The Kyokuto has proven as quick as anything on the asphalt, according to former champion, Ogisu, and that includes the British JAP and the Czechoslovakian Jawa.

A couple of Kyokuto engines have been seen outside Japan in recent times but as yet they have not made any great impression on the dirt track scene . . . although the Kyokuto was originally built for dirt speedway work.

The engine retails at around £160 and is basically a cross between a JAP and a Velocette.

It has the same stroke and bore as a JAP but features an OVERHEAD CAMSHAFT. The valve timings are approximately 10 degrees larger than on a JAP, the oil system is total loss, and the engine, which is cast iron, weighs approximately the same as a Jawa. Unusually, the magneto drive is external.

Frames, of course, differ from the normal speedway version known elsewhere, with much thicker tubing and unusual handling characteristics. Handlebars are swept backwards towards the rider with the left side slightly higher for heeling the bike over in the corners.

Riders use a steel shoe on the left which is planted on the track in similar fashion to dirt track racing.

And there you have it: Japan today—a totally unique speedway scene . . . but one that does, despite the mysticism, exist in a very big way.

Peter White is editor of the *Australian Speedway News* and the only Western journalist to have seen speedway in Japan.

There's no holding...
TIGER LOUIS

Ipswich's own champion, John 'Tiger' Louis, is surely all set for great things

FIRST DIVISION STARS ☆☆☆

Peter Collins (Belle Vue)

Nigel Boocock (Coventry)

Dave Perks (Cradley United)

Doug Wyer (Sheffield)

John Dews (Oxford)

Graeme Stapleton (Wimbledon)

PASSING IT ON
by Ivan Mauger

*One or two tips for teenager
Leslie Glover*

When I first came to ride in Britain I would have jumped at the opportunity to learn from an experienced star.

Unfortunately in those days speedway was down on its uppers—and the only opportunity I had was by listening to, and watching, Wimbledon team-mates.

But other than that there was no opportunity to spend a day or more training under an established rider.

That's one of the reasons why I launched my own series of training schools a couple of seasons ago. I'd already had a little experience of running schools for American and New Zealand riders but when I planned for my first school at Exeter in the Spring of 1971 it was the first time I'd taken a troupe of young Englishmen under my wing.

Previously I'd run a school at Belle Vue for a party of Danish youngsters—including Ole Olsen. So at least I felt my pedigree was good enough to take on this new task!

What do the youngsters learn when they come to the school? My idea is to send them away completely equipped for a speedway life.

Naturally there are some of the pupils who never get any further than the training school. But there are others who do learn—and go away and put into practice what I have told them.

24

I don't have a magic wand that can turn a no-hoper into a world-beater overnight. Of the thirty or so riders who came down to that first school at Exeter, I'd say a dozen have gone on to show drastic improvement. Another eight or so have made steady if not startling improvement.

And another ten have disappeared from the speedway scene . . . one or two of them on my advice!

What I do find terribly annoying is that there have been some riders who have paid over their tuition fee—and then treated the four day school as a joke. It's as if they've decided to pay their money to spend four days holiday with Ivan Mauger!

Last year, after the initial success of the Exeter school, I decided to expand my training school interests and had three separate schools—two at the new

Starting's so important in speedway. I demonstrate how it should be done

Talking about it—speedway students will recognise pupils Alan Sage, John Davis, Paul Palfrey and Mike Sampson

The steel shoe is an important part of a speedway star's equipment as Crewe's Dave Morton is learning. . . .

They're off. A starter's duties are never done

£200,000 track at Stoke and another at Weymouth where the stadium owner Mr. Harry Davis was most accommodating.

Perhaps the most pleasing aspect of the schools last year was the number of riders who returned for a second stint. Jack Millen, Andy Meldrum, Bob Coles, Mike Sampson, John Davis, Alan Sage and Dutch national champion Henny Kroeze all came back a second time.

One look at the way these riders improved during 1972 was, in itself, evidence of the things they had learned at Exeter twelve months earlier.

And obviously the word had got round that the schools were value-for-money as the first staging at Stoke brought a field that would have done justice to any Divison Two individual meeting.

Without giving too much away, my main aim during the early hours of the school is to sort out the basic faults in all the pupils.

Usually they fall in three simple areas and once I've given each pupil personal advice and help I can start to look further ahead and speed up the teaching process.

There are so many aspects of importance in speedway and too many people believe it is purely a case of going faster than the next man.

This isn't always the case, and besides practical instruction I try to give the pupils the theory that will help them to a better and more prosperous career.

Looking around I'm amazed at the tremendous talent there is in Britain. Certainly there's far more talent in England than any other country in the world, but so much of it is allowed to go to waste.

I know having had some of the brightest hopes at the school that all too often these riders are given no practical advice whatever, and many of the pupils had inbred faults that would prevent them ever making the very top of the tree.

Happily I was able to catch some of them early enough in their careers to give them a chance to change their basic style—but for others it was too late.

What do I get out of the training schools?

Besides the all-too-obvious answer that I make money, I also get a lot of enjoyment. Having spent fifteen years getting to the pinnacle of my speedway career I feel that I'm in the ideal situation to pass on some of the things I have learned.

And it gives me a big thrill when I pick up a morning paper to read the previous night's results—and see the name of one of my pupils as his side's top scorer.

I know then that it has all been worth while.

David Hamilton writes about...SPEEDWAY AND ME

I've always been a great sports fan. When I was at school my great ambition was to be a professional footballer. I got as far as playing for Surrey schoolboys, but when I failed a trial for my local team, Wimbledon, I realised that I just wasn't good enough to make the grade.

I still love football, watch the nearest team to me—Fulham—and play in charity matches most Sundays for the Showbiz XI.

There's practically no sport I don't enjoy. I love a game of tennis or snooker, would play more golf if only I could find time, and high on my list of favourite sports is—you've guessed it—speedway.

My introduction to speedway racing was when I was a boy. I had an Aunt who lived in North London who was crazy about it. She was 60 if she was a day, but the big excitement in her life was speed. At one time my Dad had a sports car and, whenever she was a passenger, she would plead with him to go faster. In those days—long before the 70 m.p.h. limit was introduced—she was only contented when she saw the ton up on the speedometer.

She used to take my cousin and me to see the Wembley Lions when they raced on Thursday nights. Our heroes were Tommy Price and Bill Kitchen, and in the interval we were awestruck to see a man with one leg dive about sixty feet into a huge tank of blazing oil (or was it water?).

My next association with speedway came some years later when I began my

David Hamilton

TV career with Tyne-Tees Television in Newcastle. I was compering a sports programme at the time, and we did a feature on speedway at Brough Park. It was there that I met up with Mike Parker and Reg Fearman. Another personality I remember there was Sammy Brooks, sports editor of the local paper.

Again some years lapsed before I became a speedway-goer again, though this was mainly through pressure of work. It all came about when I was playing in a charity football match in Jersey for the Showbiz XI. Another member of the team was Ed 'Stewpot' Stewart, who had been asked by Wembley to do the announcing for them on their first season back in the sport. Ed wasn't able to appear every Saturday, and asked me if I would share the announcing duties with him. Naturally, as an old fan of the sport, I was delighted. And I think I can speak for the two of us when I say that we had a fabulous time that summer.

Naturally, with two BBC disc-jockeys working together, there was a certain rivalry between us. Throughout the season there was friendly banter with promoter Bernard Cottrell about us having a race on the closing night. 'We'll go round on donkeys,' said Ed. 'We'll have a race on push-bikes,' was my suggestion. They don't call me the last of the hell-raisers for nothing!

But Bernard and Trevor Redmond would hear nothing of it. 'It's got to be the real thing or nothing,' they said, 'and we'll need two of your show business mates to make up the four.'

I don't know how we did it, but we managed to talk pop singers Leapy Lee and Troy Dante into joining us, and somehow we persuaded Ole Olsen into

Another Showbiz speedway fan is Steve McQueen, seen here with friend Barry Briggs

lending us his bike to practise on.

I don't remember much about the race, except that I kept my left foot down *all* the way round, Troy Dante fell off and I nearly ran over him, and the time-keeper said it was the slowest race in history. 78.5 was the time—and that was only the first lap!

Never again will I think speedway racing is a piece of cake—and the next time I see a rider way out in front I won't be thinking what a doddle it all is. I know because I've done it. Slowly—but I've done it.

This season I've been doing the announcing at Reading on Mond aynights. There's been some good racing at Tilehurst, and I think it's a great pity that this is yet another stadium that's to be pulled down for re-development.

As people at Romford and other venues will bear witness, speedway has its enemies. It seems a pity that some kill-joys see fit to complain about noise that happens for about two hours on one day a week, and then for only half the year.

Speedway racing fulfils a very real function. It supplies thousands of people —particularly young people—with a lot of pleasure, keeps them off the streets and provides an evening of entertainment and social contact. I'm glad to see it thriving, and I hope it goes from strength to strength in the coming years!

THE EYES HAVE IT

Here are four riders, one of whom is an odd man out. Can you say who they are, which one is odd man out and why? (Answers at the foot of the page)

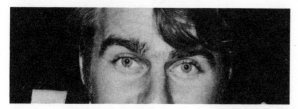

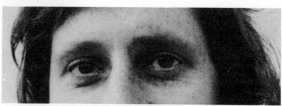

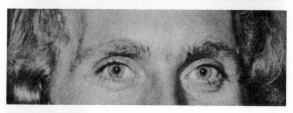

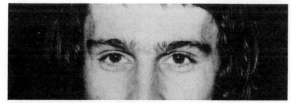

PHOTO-QUIZ ANSWERS: The riders are Odd Fossengen (Poole), Brian Collins (Poole), Terry Betts (Kings Lynn) and Mike Cake (Poole). Terry Betts is, of course, the odd man out as the other three are all team-mates at Wimborne Road.

FIRST DIVISION STARS ☆☆☆

Rick Woods (ex-Newport)

Kevin Holden (Exeter)

Sumner McKnight (ex-Swindon)

Barry Thomas (Hackney Wick)

Dave Jessup (Leicester)

FIRST DIVISION ☆☆☆ STARS

Ole Olsen (Wolverhampton)

Christer Sjosten (Coatbridge)

Eric Boocock (Halifax)

Bernie Leigh (Reading)

Pete Smith (Poole)

Ian Turner (Kings Lynn)

C

The Blossoming Jacaranda Tree
by Dick Barrie

The bright track lighting contrasts the inky black sky over the stadium and picks out the four riders moving away from the pits area to the starting gate. The shirt-sleeved crowd murmurs in anticipation and officials on the trim, lush centre green prepare for the start of the race. The scene is a familiar one to any speedway enthusiast, but the constant chirruping of the crickets in the long grass behind the pits and the heavy aroma of the purple jacaranda blossoms that drip from every branch of the trees around the arena tell the onlooker that this is not Coventry, Poole or Wimbledon he has strayed into—here speedway is staged seven thousand miles to the south of the English Channel. This is Glamis Stadium, Salisbury, Rhodesia!

Although speedway as it has developed has been raced in Australasia and Europe for close on fifty years, outside these two continents there have been only spasmodic bursts of action over the years. Following the 1939–45 war there was a general rise in interest in the sport in both America and South Africa, but these areas seemed to lose interest by the early 'fifties and activity had tailed off completely by the latter years of that decade.

Just about everyone holding an interest in speedway will know that there has been a rapid and exciting re-emergence of Californian interest in the past five years or so, but down in Africa—the fabled Dark Continent—there has been an equally encouraging re-development of speedway interest in both South Africa and Rhodesia in the 'seventies, all the more surprising perhaps when one remembers that this is a part of the world that has been steeped in political turmoil for a number of years now. Why then has this complex and addictive business of two-wheeled shale-shifting come roaring back into African popularity of late? Settle a little deeper into your armchair, put your feet on the cat, and read on . . .

The parts of Africa that had been in the main colonised by emigrants of British stock, together with many other nations, enjoyed speedway in a first wild splash of interest in 1928 or even earlier, but the bubble quickly burst at that time and it was not until the immediate post-war years that the sport was again seen by African spectators.

Renewed interest in the period from 1947–49 saw speedway gaining a foothold in Johannesburg, at the city's Wembley Stadium, but in outer regions and further north in Nyasaland and the two Rhodesias there was at this time no sign of life on the speedway front.

By 1950 there was league racing spread throughout South Africa, and riders from Britain and other Commonwealth nations were flocking to winter in the dazzling sunshine of Johannesburg and Durban, while further up country, in Southern Rhodesia, there were spasmodic meetings being staged at Bulawayo Showgrounds.

Many of the riders who sailed out from Southampton (no Boeing 747 comfort for travellers in those days!) at this time were, or would go on to become, household names on the British scene, and some—such as Barry Briggs, Ronnie Moore and Freddie Williams—would later don the World Championship crown, doubtless aided by their all-year-round racing schedule. Many young riders were to thank a winter season of sunshine speedway for the little boost their careers required to lift them above the pack in later years, but it must also be remembered that Alan Hunt and Terry Courtnell were to lose their lives while on tour, Alan as the result of a track accident and Terry in a car smash.

Sad to say however, by 1955 the sport had ebbed away in Southern Rhodesia for the time being, while squabbles between rival promotions and a worldwide depression in speedway affairs generally brought the tours to South Africa to an end the following year, leaving the Springboks only a few semi-professional meetings each year to keep a faint spark of interest flickering. One man who refused to allow the sport to die completely was veteran promoter Bob Madden who had opened up for business at his Klerksdorp (Transvaal) circuit away back in 1947 and who is still plugging away, running regular meetings for the local enthusiasts and riders, to this day!

By the time the late 'sixties happened along, speedway in Southern Africa had been virtually dead and buried for over ten years however, and when a young Scottish speedway rider named Alex Hughson took himself off on a winter's trip to Africa in a battered and tattered old van, there had been no speedway of any kind in Rhodesia for twelve or thirteen years at least. As the country had been in the world's eyes during this period of time only as a result of Prime Minister Ian Smith's dramatic declaration of independence some years before Alex's safari brought him south of the Zambesi, it is perhaps more than a little surprising that the young Hughson ever pitched up in this little-visited, if idyllic, republic set deep in the heart of the Dark Continent!

Arrive he did though, and so much did he like the country—and even then there was perhaps a dream forming at the back of his mind—that although he was to return to his native Scotland some months later to resume his business of riding speedway as a member of the Coatbridge team, it was often that his conversation would touch on matters Rhodesian and it came as little surprise to either his team-mates or his friends at home in Edinburgh when, shortly after his marriage in the closing months of 1969 to the charming Miss Sandi Vyse, Alex announced that the newly-wed Hughsons were to make a return to the land that Alex had chosen for their future—leaving Edinburgh early in 1970, again by road, in a specially-converted VW unit that was to carry them triumphantly to their destination.

On arriving in Salisbury, Alex returned to his former trade as a printer, an occupation that had supported him during his off-track moments in Scotland, but even in these early days he was already looking, asking, probing and evaluating just about every aspect of the local sporting and entertainment scene, examining the possibility of his dream—by now foremost in his mind—of bringing speedway racing, the sport he loved and so much enjoyed being part of, to his adopted country.

If Alex's emigration was little surprise, his next moves most certainly raised many an eyebrow, both in Britain and in Salisbury, when his name popped up on the agendas of local planning department courts, of Council meetings and in the columns of local press features, when the personable young Scot calmly announced his firm intention of single-handedly reviving the sport of speedway racing, not just in Salisbury—where the sport had never even been seen before —but in Bulawayo and Gwelo as well! When Alex would casually add that 'South Africa would come later' there were even more looks of amazement, but at this stage it is doubtful if the full import of his intentions was being grasped by many of his listeners.

To open a speedway track in Great Britain is obviously a costly and very

Rhodesian visitor Malcolm Brown at Matopas village, near Bulawayo

difficult task which calls for meticulous research and planning, but at least there are certain advantages for the potential promoter in the United Kingdom. For a start, there are ready supplies of willing and experienced riders with speedway equipment who can form the basis of his team, and there are established leagues for his team to apply to for membership. Not so, of course, in the Rhodesia of 1970, where Alex Hughson was quite possibly just about the only person in sight who had even HEARD of the sport, let alone envisage it running at three centres in the land within three months of the general disclosure of his plans!

Never a man to be deterred by doubters—and there were many at this time who probably were doubting his sanity, let alone his business acumen—the Edinburgh lad decided that he may as well take the bull by the horns and set up, not only his own three tracks but his own league, import the required number of riders from British League circles to staff his three teams, and—in his own words —produce 'instant speedway' from the word go! If Rhodesia was stunned, so was the British speedway scene. Advertisements soon appeared in the British press covering the sport, to offer positions on the tour to interested riders, and although there were few replies from established English riders, the younger school of British and Commonwealth men were quick to apply and on Christmas Eve of 1970, still perhaps a little unsure of exactly what they were heading into, a dozen British League riders of vastly varying experience flew out of London's Heathrow Airport into the startlingly bright sunshine of Salisbury.

While these riders were preparing for their journey, and despatching as many machines and spares as they could lay their hands on to Port Elizabeth in South Africa by boat, from there to be trucked overland to Salisbury, the promotional company set up by Alex Hughson and now embracing his two partners Andy Whyte and Ginger Grant, had won their fight with the planners and gained the blessing of Salisbury's city fathers to present the sport at the magnificent Glamis Stadium, set in the heart of the city's General Showgrounds. Options to present speedway at Bulawayo Showgrounds—scene of many a meeting in the 'fifties, but now without a trace of the original track—and at an almost derelict site in Gwelo, charmingly named the Old Newmarket Stadium, had also been taken up and construction work was in progress as tracks were laid down at all three centres in less than three weeks!

This high-speed laying of the racestrips had in itself caused crisis upon crisis, as only Alex had any real idea of what a speedway track really comprised, and the enormous importance of size, shape and surface that can make or break the spectacle of the sport for both riders and spectators. Various types of local minerals had to be tested for suitability and graded for consistency, and the construction of the three tracks proceeded in smart order to ensure readiness for the scheduled openings nights in the first week of January, 1971.

At times Alex Hughson was driving almost constantly from one town or city to the next, coaxing and cajoling his workers to the highest efforts possible in that hazy, crazy December, and there were times near the completion dates that saw him almost completely at a standstill, having worked for days and nights on end without sleep, being interviewed on Rhodesian Television at noon, driving to Bulawayo (three hundred miles to the south!) immediately after the transmission to check on track details and by early the next morning speaking to newspaper-men in Gwelo, over a hundred miles from Bulawayo!

It fell to the Salisbury centre to witness the first meeting, and although pre-match curiosity had indicated that Alex's hope for a 'gate' in excess of five thousand paying customers was not beyond the realms of possibility, the days immediately before the meeting must have been testing times for the promotion. The fateful day—January 6th of 1971—dawned at last, and an attendance of no less than 16,564 good people of Salisbury flooded into Glamis Stadium to see what this speedway caper was all about, and after the start of the meeting had been held up for fully forty-five minutes at the request of the police to allo was many spectators as possible into the ground, two Australian riders, Geoff Curtis and Bob Young, and Englishmen Graham Plant and Barry Duke roared away from the tapes in the first-ever race in the city of Salisbury! Plant raced past the chequered flag just 81.8 seconds later to win the heat, and a curious silence hung over the stadium, slowly giving way to an ever-rising buzz of excited conversation in the big crowd—they liked it!

'They' liked it at Bulawayo when Laurie Etheridge of Hackney won the trophy in their 'revival' meeting as well, and even little Gwelo—a township of less than eight thousand people—was sending over half its citizens to the Sunday afternoon meetings at Old Newmarket, where Norwegian favourite Oyvind Berg was king of the castle, in these wild, impossible days of that opening season, when Alex Hughson turned 'instant speedway' into instant success, when he and his partners ran twenty-five meetings in only fifty-nine days with only twelve riders who had previously seen speedway racing let alone ridden it, when three tracks spaced out on a three hundred mile line were brought to life from nothing, and when a grand total of over 200,000 people came into these three arenas to see what it was all about!

For the riders too, the short but so sweet trip was the making of more than a few of the young men who had been forward-thinking enough to grasp the

An unusual shot of Norway's Oyvind Berg at Gwelo

opportunity of making the trip, and riders such as Curtis, Plant, Englishman Dave Jessup and little Bobby Beaton from Scotland—all of who had been at best only reserves or second-strings with their British outfits when they set out—came romping back to start their 1971 campaigns as fully-fledged headleaders! Scottish novice Jim Gallacher had his first real taste of team racing on this trip as well, and Bob Young was another rider to benefit hugely from wintering in the hot sunshine of Africa at this time.

Understandably flushed with his successes, Alex Hughson refused to rest on his laurels in any way and planned a bigger and better season for the following British close season, even making a short trip home to cast his eyes over the latest crop of young riders and the newer methods of speedway presentation at the more go-ahead B.L. centres.

In spite of his careful background preparation and the engagement of a vastly more experienced squad of riders to re-staff the three sides, little good was to come of this second season of sunshine speedway however, despite the careful groundwork by the promotion.

Shortly before his season opened, Alex Hughson sat down and explained to me that, as he had carefully selected the most competent riders for his purpose to set up the teams alongside the rising crop of young Rhodesians who had flocked into the sport after the opening series of meetings (one of whom, Peter Prinsloo, had even gone so far as to travel to Britain that summer and had shown remarkable progress in a short spell while riding in the colours of both Wembley and Ipswich) and as he had carefully blended into his promotion every proven ingredient that appeared to have found success in Britain that year, only what he termed an 'unforeseen disaster' could prevent Rhodesian speedway from blossoming even more brightly in this second season of its rebirth.

Disaster was right! The earlier Hughson jest about 'instant speedway' backfired on him with a vengeance when Alex discovered the one thing that one could not do with his 'instant' product—add water!

The heaviest, most unexpected and most frequent rains in over seventy years swept Rhodesia—nearly always on speedway nights—that season, cancelling eight meetings from the schedule and affecting an amazing twenty-three out of the remaining thirty meetings on the fixture lists, although these meetings could at least be staged. Attendances plummetted, for the average Rhodesian will just not budge from his home if he feels that rain is even threatening, and the second season ended with an air of gloom—although not of despondancy— hanging over the promotion, who were punctilious about the settlement of every commitment made to each of the touring riders, despite their heavy operating losses over the term.

For the riders on this tour, the weather must have been about the only disappointment however, as once again the trip proved that Rhodesia was the place for a rider to 'find himself' and return to Britain an improved young man. Jessup took another huge leap forward on this trip, and Scottish youngster Brian Collins was another who was a much improved shale-shifter on his taking to track in Poole's colours in 1972. The red-haired Australian Bluey Valentine was able to clinch a full team place at Sheffield by courtesy of his Gwelo rides on this trip, and scrambler Tom Leadbitter almost set the Midlands aflame by his immediate success in Wolverhampton on flying home.

Alex Hughson faced problems at this stage of course, but few Scots are defeatists and Alex merely sat down and thought hard on the subject of the future—and paid the first of several visits over the Limpopo to South Africa to check up on the state of closed-circuit motor sport in the former dominion. Although speedway had of course long since faded from South Africa's big-city arenas, stock-car racing was still hauling in impressive crowds, and Alex decided that he could perhaps afford to re-examine his policies in the light of this information.

Why not, argued Alex to himself, rethink our programmes along the lines that have proved successful in Australia and New Zealand for so many years and combine the interests of our regular speedway supporter and his stock-car cousin, with perhaps some midget-car racing and sidecar events thrown in? Although it was a blow to abandon his bikes-only meetings at this stage—and he himself admits that, with the better weather that was experienced the following season, there may well have still been a full market for solo speedway without the addition of the cars—Alex has always tried to remember that a promoter's first concern should be for his public, not his pocket, and if the average Rhodesian spectator has now become accustomed to watching both cars and bikes in one meeting, that is quite all right with Mr Hughson!

Following the close of that second, rainsoaked, season that squelched to a halt in the (British) spring of 1972, Alex and his long-time buddy Roni Ferguson (a former Edinburgh junior rider who had emigrated to Rhodesia in 1971 and has since then carved himself quite a reputation on track as a rider with a tremendous will to win under Rhodesian conditions), set about the long and difficult business of converting first the Salisbury track and fittings, then those at Bulawayo, to dual-purpose arenas that could cater equally for cars and bikes.

41

To build a safety fence that is strong enough to halt a two-ton car in full flight, yet that is still within the stringent and very necessary safety regulations that are required for the full protection of solo speedway riders, is not without its problems and the twosome expounded the various requirements time and again to their workforces at the two circuits to ensure that all was in order. Finally all the work was completed, and Alex was once again rewarded by five-figured attendances at both the tracks when he reopened his programmes with the mixed car and bike events, although by this time it was clear that, with the passing of the speedway league that had been one of the prime reasons for its inception in the first place, the Gwelo track must fall by the wayside.

Once again, all was well on the Rhodesian speedway front, and since that time the sport has continued to flourish as the main two-wheeled nation in Africa, with Prinsloo now receiving challenges for his twice-won National Championship title from such rapidly-improving youngsters as 21-year-old Pip Harris, both of whose brothers are also experienced riders, and 17-year-old Mike Ferreira. The British League boys still come a-calling each close-season, and the place must definitely hold some attraction, for the lanky Bob Young and Scotsman Jimmy Gallacher have now made the trip no less than three times!

If the reintroduction of speedway to Rhodesia was of an immediate nature, the sport's more recent—and to date more modest—comeback further south in South Africa has been a more gradual process. The solid perseverance of Bob Madden at Klerksdorp had kept just a spark alive since the 'fifties of course, and a team of sorts had even been recruited at Klerksdorp by the fomer English star Dennis Newton (who had emigrated to Johannesburg a decade earlier), and had made a short tour of the Rhodesian tracks early in 1971. Although they suffered huge defeats each time out the potential of at least one young man—named Ettienne Olivier—had stood out clearly.

In the cities the former circuits had all been tarmac-covered to cater for the cars however, and this seemed to be the greatest drawback to the Hughson-inspired African revival spreading south. Alex Hughson is one determined young man however, and following several trips over the border to discuss matters with various organisations in South Africa, he won over an important ally late in 1972 when he finally persuaded the doyen of South African promoters, veteran Buddy Fuller, of the viability of the running of speedway again, and Buddy—never a man to do things by halves, it seems—promptly ripped up the tar at his three main venues, at Johannesburg's Wembley Stadium, the Alan Ford Stadium at Durban's Hoy Park and the Dunswart Arena at Benoni, relaying all three with shale

American Champion Rick Woods in action at Johannesburg's Wembley Stadium

to give speedway a fair run, albeit in mixed meetings alongside the proven attraction of cars.

Fuller had several advantages that had been denied to his Rhodesian counterparts when they had commenced operations, in that he already had a nucleus

of local riders from the Klerksdorp venue from which he could build up a programme of events, and he had in Rhodesia a neighbouring country from which
he could 'borrow' visiting star men to make relatively inexpensive 'one-night-
stands' at his tracks, and it was in this manner that the re-establishment of big-
city speedway in South Africa was undertaken.

Following the obvious delight of his patrons at the presentation of two-
wheeled racing again, Fuller contacted Alex Hughson and set up a series of
unofficial Test matches at his circuits between South Africa and Rhodesia, a
series which saw the home side heavily defeated by a visiting squad that was just
a little too experienced and fresh from regular, hard racing, but it was this series
—which incidentally saw the return to the saddle of promoter Hughson—that
really proved the viability of top-grade speedway on the Springbok tracks.

The South African authorities were anxious to consolidate the position that
speedway had gained in the public eye through the Tests with Rhodesia, but every
effort to engage a touring side with British connections was to prove in vain,
despite numerous rumours having done their annual rounds in England that 'this
year a SA trip *was* on at last', and promoter Fuller, tiring perhaps of the lack of
British action over such a tour possibility, pulled the very boldest of strokes by
coolly inviting over the best four-man American side he could engage on a four-
week tour!

*Rhodesian Stock Car Champion Eddy McNamara (left) and exiled Scot Roni
Ferguson—one of the country's top speedway stars—visit a Salisbury
Children's Home*

44

The Yanks, led by their National Champion Rick Woods and with young Mike Curuso being backed up by Sumner McKnight and the blond-haired Scott Autrey, both of whom joined Woods in British League racing in 1973, were far too strong for the South Africans but the tour was a wild success. Ground records were broken at both Wembley and Durban, and when near the end of their stay the Americans were matched in an individual competition with several of the British League riders that had been imported by Alex Hughson for action on the Rhodesian tracks, the Springbok spectators were at last able to realise just how good speedway could be.

All the American youngsters proved to be excellent and superb showmen as well as skilful riders, with Woods the standout on both counts. The fact that they were all able to collect such good results in competition with British-based riders of fair quality could well have influenced Autrey, McKnight and Woods in the decision they later undertook to do the British season instead of their domestic one the following summer, while the progress shown by a couple of South Africans in the series has also prompted Etienne Olivier and Danie Fourie to seek further experience in Europe since that time.

Following the departure of the U.S. riders, the Dunswart circuit was again surfaced with tarmac, but with both Hoy Park and Wembley going from strength to strength on the solo side, and with enthusiasm also building up for the solo sections at some of the other up-country circuits such as Klerksdorp, it seems that —like their Rhodesian neighbours—the South Africans can look forward to a further lease of life for the sport in their country, and with careful management and promotion, and an absence of exploitation, there is little reason why speedway cannot at this point in time look forward to a much longer lifespan in both South Africa and Rhodesia than it has previously been allowed to enjoy in previous instances. Certainly the complete sellout in attendance at Durban for the Final of the 1973 South African Championship, eventually won by the experience of the veteran Dennis Newton from Scot Jimmy Gallacher and Rhodesia's Peter Prinsloo, must give the Springbok speedfans every confidence that the sport is now back in their land to stay!

Having thus surveyed the scene in both African countries in which speedway is currently staged—and with the possible exception of Angola, it seems likely these are the only two in which the sport is ever likely to be staged in the foreseable future—we can thus look forward to the future of the game in Southern Africa. The continuing absence from all forms of motor sport of the political issues that have clouded African sport for some time now is of course a blessing, and one which we can only hope will remain in speedway's favour. The sport is flourishing in Southern Africa, and the continuing emergence of further local talent to join the men who have already shown natural ability within a short space of time, will no doubt assist local interest yet further.

Young riders such as the truly remarkable Prinsloo in Rhodesia, as well as his previously-mentioned rivals Harris and Ferreira, and the younger set of South Africans led by Olivier and backed up by the Fourie brothers and Tommy Fox—all of whom have benefited hugely from the visits to their tracks of Alex Hughson's riders from British circuits each year—are now taking over the mantles worn for so long in South Africa by the ageing, although still effective, Newton, Neil Mortimer and Des Haswell, and the experiences in Europe of Olivier and Danie Fourie in the summer of 1973 can only accelerate the progress of this duo still further.

The British-based visitors have continued to use their holidays in the African sun to advantage as well, and all the riders who have so far wintered in Rhodesia can confirm that neither republic is a strife-torn battlefield or a dictator-repressed peasant colony. More likely that they will tell of a pleasant, sun-soaked paradise, where the strain of the constant hurly-burly of British League racing can be washed away, and riding techniques improved upon under less pressure than they might normally expect to find while racing at home, or even in Australia or New Zealand, where again the all-round standards are higher, and the pressures greater.

When Alex Hughson had his dream, there were many doubters as I have said. Today one can point to the success of the reintroduction of speedway to two large countries, both many thousands of miles from their nearest speedway-racing neighbours, in which it is virtually as a direct result of that doubted dream that the sport flourishes today—for although Alex is not directly involved in the promotion of the sport in South Africa, the revival there would and could never have taken place other than as a direct result of the Hughson 'instant' miracle over the Limpopo a couple of years earlier. It would indeed be pleasant to think that at some point in the future, the ruling bodies of the sport in one or other country might find it possible in some way to reward Hughson for the part he has played—a starring role, to be sure—in the phoenix-like rise of speedway from the grave into which it had been flung in the mid-fifties.

A final thought on the African revival is, that although so far it has been British-based riders who have benefited most—both financially and in experience—from their Rhodesian winters, in the past South Africa provided two World

An historic picture: the field for the 1972 Rhodesian Championship, the first time a multi-national line-up has fought out the title

Finalists in Henry Long, who ran 8th in 1952 while attached to Belle Vue, and Birmingham clubman Doug Davies (13th in 1956), and if the standard of racing and competition in Africa can continue to rise in the manner that has already been experienced in three or so years, then there can be no earthly reason why Prinsloo, Ferreira or Olivier, given sufficient encouragement and overseas competition, cannot rise to emulate the achievements of their famous predecessors—all have the natural ability, all that has so far been lacking is the prolonged experience and opportunity of tackling top-class opposition abroad.

Dick Barrie is Scotland's foremost speedway journalist, and a regular visitor to the African continent.

SECOND ★★★ DIVISION STARS

Chris Bailey (Barrow)

Mark Perram (ex-Berwick)

George Major (Birmingham)

Arthur Price (Boston)

★★★SECOND DIVISION STARS

Bobby McNeil (Eastbourne)

Ray Hassall (Chesterton)

Ian Gills (ex-Ellesmere Port)

Dave Piddock (Canterbury)

D

A DAY WITH IVAN MAUGER

Racing in America—on the long track

Life can be tough at the bottom!

But it can be a darned sight tougher at the top!

Paradoxical though it may be, for every worry that the kid has with one foot on the bottom rung of the ladder there are half a dozen problems for the King at the top.

Certainly life is far, far busier at the top. Ask Ivan Mauger. Or Ole Olsen. Or Barry Briggs. Or any of the true world class performers.

And life doesn't start the minute they wheel a new Jawa off the trailer. Or end the moment they climb out of the shower after a meeting.

It goes on near 24 hours a day. Take a typical day in the life of Ivan Mauger.

It begins, usually, round about seven in the morning when the alarm goes and sets off the automatic tea-maker (a second half prize at a Belle Vue meeting incidentally) to begin the day on a sweet note.

Before the eight o'clock news the New Zealander is usually dressed and having grabbed a couple of pieces of toast prepares to take his youngest daughter Debbie to school in the car.

Once he's back at home there's several hours of hard business to be done. A room of their five-bedroomed house in fashionable Bramhall, the Cheshire suburb where his close neighbours have included Manchester United's tempestuous Georgie Best, has been converted into an office with pine-panelled walls.

50

The ivory telephone seems to beat out a constant concerto and Mauger hastily scribbles notes to remember on a National Provident Insurance pad.

It's from here that he arranges the business side of his speedway life. At least twice a day he's in touch with his fellow directors of his Project-A-Sport Company, originally launched to capitalise on his World Championship success but now involved in far more than that.

Business is brisk at Project-A-Sport and he needs all his wits about him to keep *au fait* with the happenings in New Zealand, Australia and on the American Continent.

Son Kym gets the hang of his Yamaha scrambler

Off duty: Ivan Mauger and his wife Raye (holding lamb) at a Young Farmer's function

Once his morning's business is over he can prepare himself for the real task at hand—that of riding speedway. Germany and the Western European countries command much of his time as he arranges with his German agent his regular week-end jaunts to the long grass and sand track meetings.

Having become the first World Long Track Champion he's upped the anti for all his Continental meetings but even at a minimum of £500 a throw there is no lack of takers.

Several times a week 33-year-old Mauger must travel the twenty-odd miles over the rugged Derbyshire peaks to see ace tuner Guy Allott in his Buxton workshops.

It is here that the pair of them put their heads together and ensure that every time Mauger gently throttles his 500 c.c. Jawa to the tapes it is in peak condition.

Like an athlete a speedway bike must never be one degree below. If it is that can mean points lost . . . and in speedway points lost hits where it hurts most —the pocket!

It is probably fair to say that Ivan doesn't spend as much time on his bikes today as he did eight years ago. Then he had to do all the work himself. He'd cut the tyres. Wash out the carburettor. Clean the wheels. And do the one hundred and one little things that need doing between meetings.

Today he can afford to employ a full-time mechanic to do those things although he still supervises most of the work and still trusts only himself to do some of the more delicate matters.

Even so most of his afternoon is chewed up by the driving need to ensure that his bike is as near perfect as human frailty will allow.

Evenings—those when he is not riding and during the summer they are few and far between—are usually spent helping the children with their homework . . . having the occasional game of Monopoly or Cluedo with the kids . . . or just sitting down and relaxing in front of the colour television.

Rarely though can he spend an uninterrupted evening watching the box. As in the day, the telephone is never silent.

It could be Briggo ringing about plans for an American trip. It might be Reg Fearman wanting to confirm an open booking.

Or any number of other people. All demanding his attention.

Life at the top may be fine. But only if you don't weaken. . . .

H.R.H. Princess Anne listens to a speech by Ivan Mauger at the Daily Express 'Sportsman of the Year' Banquet last year

Ivan signs a new contract with sponsors TT Leathers under the watchful eye of the company's managing director, Mr. Len Thwaites

The picturesque scenery at Germany's Ruhpolding track

DIGGERLAND~ THEN AND NOW
by Peter White

Despite Australia's lack of success in the World Championship sphere for more than two decades, the nation remains one of the world's leading speedway powers —if only for the intense activity centred Down Under during the European close-season.

Other Southern Hemisphere countries operate during the period October to March—mainly South Africa, Rhodesia and New Zealand—but it's Australia where it's all at.

Australia instituted the revival of the Test series against Great Britain in 1967.

And Australia remains responsible for their continuation.

Australia inaugurated the Australasian tour of a full seven man Swedish international squad in 1971–72 and, the same season, became the first country to recognise the return of America to the international speedway scene by inviting a full scale Yankee side to the Antipodes.

When the shutters go up on the British League season in October the dedicated professionals turn their thoughts to winter racing—and to Australasia.

The island Continent generally has more prevalent pickings, although New Zealand is equally popular in some quarters.

However, it's Aussie that concerns us in this chapter and in Diggerland today the speed scene looms bigger, better and brighter than for many years.

Australia . . . the country where the sport first kicked off almost fifty years ago.

54

*Australia's last World Champion
. . . Jack Young in West Ham's
colours*

Australia . . . provider of the first-ever World Champion—Lionel Van Praag in 1936—and the first rider to annex the crown twice in succession: Jack Young in 1951 and 1952.

Australia . . . land of sun, sand, sea . . . and *speedway*.

A country where, at home in our own backyard, it's all happening. Yet, in the eyes of Europe, a mere sunshine *playground* now striving desperately to regain past glories.

Undeniably Australia has slipped from grace on the European scene. But the Kangaroos are still in there fighting, as witnessed by their success in the pilot 1972 Inter-Nations Tournament and the appearance of Sydney star, Jim Airey, in the 1971 World Individual Final and World Team Championship (when he represented Great Britain!).

And the push is on to continue the progress, with seemingly more and more youngsters each year heading overseas—all with that magical twinkle of the World Crown in their eyes.

At the same time Australia's stocks back home are high. In their own country the Kangaroos have proven capable of tweaking the tail of any international opposition.

Last summer (1971–72) they dispensed with the allegedly super-Swedes from Scandinavia by six matches to one in the seven series internationals. And that was against a team which included only two riders who had never appeared in a World Final.

55

This season (1972–73) Australia walloped Great Britain to the same tune, 6–1. This shows just what Aussie is capable of when the strongest available teams are fielded. Several sides in the past have been somewhat suspect but this year no such accusations could be levelled and to add weight to the feat the Kangaroos achieved the result without the services of their number one, Jim Airey, in five of the seven Tests.

Airey fractured a wrist in a fall from a mini-bike while teaching children to ride a week after the first Test. The injury was the most serious of his versatile motorcycling career to date!

So we have what could well be termed, relatively, a boom period for solo motorcycles in a speedway sphere where their very existence is constantly threatened by many other popular forms of racing such as sidecars, midget speedcars and the new rage of the country, production sedans.

Sedans, which are late-model road models stripped and tuned for high speed racing as opposed to the old stock-car idea, are rapidly snowballing in popularity and prestige across Australia at present.

But . . . and savour the thought . . . the solos are matching them stride for stride and continue to form the basic diet of programmes at all the major tracks from coast to coast.

While the battle between sections for supremacy Down Under is never-ending, the solos retain their staid supporters, relying as always on pure, clean-cut thrills and unsurpassed human skills.

Unfortunately the vast distances of the Continent prohibit regular team racing and riders become isolated to their particular home town or city.

This leads to groups of competitors of varying ability, from international aces down to rank novices, and thus handicapping is necessary to maintain interest.

Handicapping is a necessary evil, being to Australasian speedway what league racing is to British speedway.

It puts the riders on equal terms and gives the public value for money. Although, to be fair, it is fraught with dangers for the riders.

The solo ranks in all Australian states, with the exception of Tasmania and Northern Territory, are presently thriving. From east to west each capital city has its glut of star men . . . and in between more and more new international-class tracks are appearing.

On the west coast there is the long-established Claremont speedway in Perth—the mecca of racing in Western Australia.

It is the home of such notables as Chum and Glyn Taylor, the father and son team now riding at Second Division Crewe; Les Sharpe (Halifax) and many others including the inevitable stay-at-homers of international calibre whose class should not be dismissed simply because they choose not to journey to Europe, such as Bob O'Leary.

Recently a new track opened at Bunbury, about one hundred miles away on the sea coast, and the indications are that this will further foster solo competition.

Across the 'dead heart' of Australia—a 1,500 mile trek along a mud track appropriately named the Nullarbor Plain—is Adelaide and the renowned Rowley Park speedway under the promotion of colourful character, Kym Bonython.

Rowley . . . the home of National Champion, John Boulger, and former great, Jack Young. A quarter-mile circuit commonly regarded as the Aussie bowl most conducive to top flight solo racing.

Further afield in South Australia are located several 'country' circuits which are invaluable as training grounds for many of tomorrow's stars—places such as Murray Bridge, where former Cradley Heath rider Chris Bass now lives, Renmark, and Whyalla.

Across the border in Victoria, things are throbbing with a new track at

Current Australian National Champion John Boulger

Australian Test Captain and former National Champion Jim Airey

picturesque Warnnambool rapidly entering into calculations for major events.

Warnnambool, promoted by a local car club, leaves little to be desired from the solo viewpoint and some top-rate matches have already been staged there.

The appearance of the British Lions Test team has seen the place packed to capacity . . . which proves that Aussie speedway interest is not merely confined to the capital cities along the coastline.

Melbourne, of course, claims the major raceway in the suburb of Brooklyn, and other tracks which use solos in Victoria are Bendigo, where poor Jack Biggs rode his last race, and Mildura, whose most famous speedway son is the new Aussie golden boy, Phil Crump.

The capital of Australia, Canberra, was for many years completely devoid of speedway action. Recently the Tralee track was constructed a few miles out of town and this now lays claim to being one of the most successful in the land.

Canberra, the seat of the nation where Parliament, and many thousands of public servants are housed, has long offered an open invitation for entertainment in the speedway mould. The patrons flock in and so another venue has been cultivated for the many young riders from the Sydney area who are desperately trying to get a break.

Enjoying his second season in Britain is Wimbledon's Neil Cameron

Jim Ryman in action back at home

Start at Con Migro's Claremont Speedway, Perth. From left: Bob O'Leary, Rod Chessell,
Chum Taylor, Abe Schneider, Malcolm Simmons, Ivan Mauger

Ironically, in Sydney there are too many riders for too few opportunities. But it is fair to say that if a rider shows just a flicker of promise, he'll get every chance to make good. Keen observers are continually on the look-out for likely talent and you can be sure it won't remain stifled for long.

Basically a Sydney speedway show can use a maximum of only 21 riders per meeting. With more than 60 on the books of the SRA (Speedway Riders Association) there are inevitably disappointments, especially in the light of the tendency of Liverpool to swing more and more to the cars.

The city of Sydney, the largest and fairest in Australia, houses two major tracks—the Showground Speedway Royale, only a few miles from the city centre, and Liverpool, an out-of-town track approximately 20 miles west but still very much in the suburban area.

Liverpool made its mark with international solo racing, thanks largely to the efforts of the indefatigable late, great, Gordon Guasco, but latterly the trend has been towards the cars.

In the summer recently concluded, the Showground became the venue for three Australia–Great Britain Tests, the New South Wales Championship, and the Australian National Championship Grand Final (won by John Boulger).

Strangely, a feeling has emerged amongst some Sydney riders that too much experience on the fast third-of-a-mile Showground track will hamper their subsequent progress overseas should they make the trip and thus they've developed a reluctance to turn out at the renowned Royale.

Nigel Boocock, I think, provided the answer by slating this idea and pointing to the immaculate Jim Airey, who was literally 'bred' on the Showground and is still the 'Master' on this one particular track, but who has shown few ill-effects for it in his career in Britain.

So it is still the Sydney Showground where the solos provide the Saturday night speedway spectacle after beginning under the Johnnie Hoskins banner way back in 1925.

To the south of Sydney, at the steel port of Kembla, near Wollongong, is the 'Rye House' of NSW speedway—Kembla Grange.

Here the newcomer gets his chance.

Prize money is meagre, the track is rough, crowds are small, the circuit is difficult . . . but it's always one heck of a Sunday afternoon out and if a rider can make good at Kembla (where he gets every opportunity) then he should have few further worries. He will then know he has ability . . . and with luck it should lead to a breakthrough into the Sydney big-time.

To the north of Sydney is the newest track to make an impression Down Under—at Newcastle, another steel port some 100 miles up the coast. Named Jerilderie Park, this is another international class circuit which has rather miraculously been carved from virgin scrub virtually overnight. On an impulse, after seeing a Test match in Sydney, the directors decided to build a speedway and run a show.

Build a speedway they certainly did.

They now possess one of the most magnificently appointed grounds in Australia—for a speedway constructed completely from scratch.

And, more importantly, unlike some other new out-of-town tracks they are concentrating on the bikes as the bulk of the programme.

The Newcastle area has been recognised as a hot-bed of motoryele talent for some time and, in fact, it was from the coalfields of Maitland, Cessnock and Newcastle that the original leg-trailing stars such as Billy Lamont emerged.

Today's best known rider from the Newcastle area is flame-haired Sheffield Tiger, Bob Valentine.

In a matter of months new prospects have emerged from Jerilderie Park—the brightest being Don Howison—and by March Newcastle was strong enough to challenge successfully the Sydney Showground to an impromptu teams match.

Novice Jim Gossen rides outside fellow Aussie Dave Mills at an Australian training track

Many hundred miles further north again is the sunshine state of Queensland which is probably the strongest solo state in Australia at present.

In Brisbane, internationals abound. And they all fly around the Exhibition Ground slick little quarter-miler. Names like Jack White, Kevin Torpie, Steve Reinke, John Titman, Doug White and Bryan Loakes are as common to the sporting public of Brisbane as your Bobby Moores and Bobby Charltons are to Londoners and Mancunians.

And just to keep their hand in, they have the opportunity of riding at Ipswich, about 30 miles out of town, as well.

One interesting feature of the Exhibition Ground programmes is the way it caters for novice solo riders . . . progressive thinking by manager Bill Goode who is obviously only too aware of cultivating riders for the future. There they stage a junior teams match prior to the programme proper every meeting.

Queensland, of course, is a large state and working still further north towards Cape York, one finds solo hot-beds at Bundaberg, Rockhampton, Townsville, Ayr and now Cairns.

Although the standards at these centres are not as high as in the capitals, they are nevertheless a valuable contribution to the Australian speedway scene.

A scene which, joyously, is thriving like never before.

Looking Back at the Kiwis
by ALAN CLARK

Speedway began in New Zealand way back in 1929 when they opened the doors at the English Park track in Christchurch—cradle of the champions.

But to many New Zealand fans they'll never see racing on the South Island. Instead, their shale activity is confined to New Zealand's North Island.

Rarely do riders from the two islands come together—unless it is for the New Zealand Championship, a test match . . . or when they meet up in Britain!

To try and trace the story of speedway racing on the North Island we asked writer Alan Clark—formerly a sidecar performer himself—to prepare a brief history.

He's done that and provided, for the first time ever in a British publication, a run-down of the New Zealand championship since its early days when Alf Mattson became the 1930 title-holder.

There are still several early gaps in the complete list—but no-one anywhere seems to be able to fill in those gaps.

While speedway was being launched on the South Island, Kilbirnie Stadium, Wellington, opened its doors to the paying patrons as long ago as March 9th, 1929.

It was a new sport. No-one knew whether it would catch on and Australian Max Graham was brought over to show the locals what it was all about.

He had no real local opposition and was virtually unbeaten at Kilbirnie. But he proved one thing: the locals would pay to watch speedway racing and crowds were healthy by the time Kilbirnie opened for its second season the following November. First real local discovery was Wally Kilminster who was later to make a big name for himself in England at Wembley Stadium.

Flushed with the success of racing at Kilbirnie the New Zealand promoters began scouring the North Island to try and find other suitable venues.

By the end of the year we had seen the opening of the Western Springs

One of the world's first Test Matches: the English Test Team 1936. Left to right: Stan Greatrex, Wally Clibbert, Ron Harrison and Eric Langton

Stadium. On Saturday 30th November the stadium was officially opened by the then Mayor, Mr. Geirge Baildon, before a packed-house 15,000 crowd.

High on the bill of fare was the visit of Australians Syd Perkins and Arthur Mann who had travelled across from Christchurch where they had been thrilling the crowds.

Western Springs was a brand new stadium that had cost £24,500 to build and to this day it is the only track in New Zealand that has stayed open to speedway through the years.

Among the riders on that first night were Len Coulthard—who chalked up the most successes riding a Rex Acme machine—and Alf Mattson who was mounted on a Norton.

Alf was to become one of New Zealand's early stars and he carried off the first-ever New Zealand championship when it was staged at Kilbirnie Speedway on 26th March, 1930.

Other early visitors to New Zealand included Bill Stiepewich and Les Lawrence from Australia and on February 19th there was a visitor with a difference—Auckland welcomed Miss Fay Taylour on her New Zealand debut.

A larger than usual crowd turned out to watch her have a special match race series against Auckland rider Bill Herbert. No quarter was asked or given and Miss Taylour won the first clash; Bill took the second; and Miss Taylour clinched it in the third when Bill overdid things trying to catch his opponent.

63

It was in the 1930–31 season that team racing obtained its first footing in New Zealand with a team of six riders arriving for a series of special match races and four official test matches at Auckland, Wellington, Christchurch and Dunedin.

The first meeting took place in Wellington with the Australian squad skippered by the then reigning Queensland State champion Jack Bishop. Matched against him and his team was a local side captained by Wally Kilminster.

The locals ran out winners by 30–24 points in an exciting meeting on 17th January . . . and it helped establish team racing as a popular form of speedway.

For the record the Wellington team on that occasion was: Wally Kilminster (Rudge), Clarrie Tonks (Douglas), Tim Wilkinson (Harley), Bill Harvie (Douglas), Eddie Naylor (Rudge) and Stan Palmer (Douglas).

The Australians fielded this side: Jack Bishop (Rudge), Cyril Anderson (Rudge), Harold Stevens (Rudge), Eric Whittle (Douglas), Bert Jones (Rudge) and Eric Hamberger (Douglas).

Speedway had grabbed hold of the New Zealand population and they heralded the arrival of popular English star Squib Burton when he sailed in to set up a new four-lap record at Wellington on his first outing in New Zealand towards the end of January, 1930. A fortnight later he lowered his own record from 78 seconds to 76.6 seconds—the fastest competition time recorded in New Zealand at that time.

Squib's immense popularity and skill paved the way to the introduction of test matches between England and New Zealand with the first clash between the two countries slated for Dunedin on 18th February, 1931. The English boys proved far too strong at Dunedin and ran out convincing 36–18 winners, going on to win the series 3–0 with further wins at Kilbirnie and Auckland.

Led by the immaculate Squib Burton the English side—Norman Evans, Frank Bond, George Greenwood, Jim Kempster and Roger Frogley—did much to lay the foundations of the successful future of speedway in the Islands and helped show the locals the standard of racing on the other side of the world.

It was then that New Zealanders realised they would have to broaden their horizon and start travelling to Australia and England if they were to be able to match the overseas visitors on their own tracks.

But all was not well in New Zealand at that time. With the depression hitting and a big credit squeeze sweeping through the country Kilbirnie found the running costs were getting too great and had to close down.

This left only Auckland and Christchurch to see out the season with visitors

Ton Farndon (Jap), Nobby Key (Jap), Roger Frogley (Jap), Jack Jackson (Rudge) and Vic Huxley (Rudge) sharing most of the honours between them.

Despite hints that it might not re-open Auckland's Western Springs track bade welcome to the 1932–33 season on November 26, 1932 and ran a series of twelve weekly meetings until 25th February. Again England riders took the opportunity of spending the winter in the softer climate of New Zealand with Eric Langton, Nobby Key, Tiger Stephenson, Wally Phillips and Eric Gregory making the trip by boat. And from America came Ray Tauser to add to the overseas opposition.

Twelve months earlier New Zealand fans—and racers—had seen their first glimpse of the English-made Jap engine and they clamoured for them. By the time Western Springs finished its season local riders Mattson, Charlie Goldberg and Mich Silich were mounted on them.

There was no speedway at all during 1934 but promoters decided they could take another gamble in 1935 and both Auckland and Wellington re-opened their doors. However at neither centre did speedway recapture its former appeal and both operated low-key seasons. It was a similar story the following season although crowds improved considerably with the visit of a host of famous speedway names.

From America came trick rider Putt Mossman, Pee Wee Cullem, Bo Lisman, Sam Arena, Byrd McKinney, Ray Grant and Manuel Trujillo. From England came Eric Langton, Bob Harrison, Bill Clibbert and Stan Greatrex. And from Australia came Dicky Case and Lionel Van Praag.

Two of New Zealand's best—Ronnie Moore and Ron Johnston in 1952

Brothers Mick and Laurie Holland

E

The riders split up into small groups and interchanged between the three tracks operating—Auckland, Wellington and Christchurch.

It wasn't only speedway that was on the race programme. At the fourth meeting of the season at Auckland—date: January 11, 1936—the main publicised feature was the appearance of the Putt Mossman Motor-cycle Rodeo. It should have been a glorious occasion with Mossman performing a blindfold jump over his wife Helen.

It didn't work out like that. Putt missed the ramp and ran into Helen who was rushed off to Auckland Hospital. Fortunately it wasn't as serious as it looked and she was soon up and about . . . and joining in Putt's one-man circus!

Putt obviously liked New Zealand and he returned the following year, ostensibly to Auckland where a bunch of enthusiasts had banded together to form the Auckland Speedway Club to run their own meetings. Mainly though it was a couple of races—and the rest of the show given over to the Putt Mossman Show.

While he was here Putt took over promoting his own shows at Palmerstone North and when the Wellington company ceased to operate at Kilbirnie he took over that track too.

No-one could claim that speedway was in a healthy state as the thirties rolled towards a depressing conclusion. A quick run-down of the seasons immediately before the war bear this out:

1937–38. First appearance in New Zealand of midget car racing. A team of Americans under the management of Roscoe Turner visited Western Springs and started the ball rolling. It's been a mixed solo and cars programme ever since. The usual programme was nine car races and six solos.

1938–39: Only ten local riders at Auckland with a mixed programme. The season lasted for eight meetings.

1939–40: Nine meetings at Auckland. Programme was two heats and a final repeated, which meant six races only.

1940–41: Ten meetings in the final season before hostilities forced all speedways to close. On the final night of the season Charlie Buchanan became New Zealand Champion.

It wasn't until the war drew to its close that speedway opened up again in Auckland with Western Springs being first on to the bandwagon with a meeting on December 23rd, 1944.

The thought of speedway two days before Christmas might not appeal to English fans but the warm summer weather (and possibly the end of the war) brought the crowds flocking, shirt-sleeved, to the track and it was quite a successful season which seemed to ensure speedway's future at The Springs.

Solos began to recapture their former appeal and within a couple of seasons were outnumbering the cars. Spurred on by the success of the sport at Western Springs, the North Island gained its second post-war track in 1947 when Palmerston North was opened as a genuine speedway. Early in 1948 the sport returned to Wellington. Not at Kilbirnie, but this time at Lower Hutt where the crown prince of New Zealand speedway, Bruce Abernethy, was to pick up a big local following.

Speedway had found a new footing on the North Island and inter-city team racing was introduced in the 1948–49 season with matches between tracks at Auckland, Wellington, Palmerston and Christchurch.

English riders again took up the challenge and became regular visitors . . . although promoters had learned from a mistake in the early days: too many foreign stars had then flooded the tracks and in so doing forced out local talent. While that didn't matter too much in the height of the season it left fans wanting much better entertainment when the English, Australian and American riders left New Zealand and returned home.

It was because of this that it was decided to introduce a new curtailment on overseas riders and they were limited to one per track. Inter-city racing was an immediate hit and the Canterbury team—based at Christchurch—walked away

Two of the stars of the past—
Ron Mason and Les Moore
(Ronnie's father)

The 1950 South Island Team: Kevin Hayden, Ernie Browne, Jack Cunningham, Geoff Mardon and Ronnie Moore

with the series.

Because of the travel problems involved all teams were restricted to four riders and it was agreed that matches would be decided on an aggregate total with home and away meetings over eight heats. Canterbury, led by England's Norman Parker, beat Auckland convincingly 63–33; and Wellington by the same score. Even though they lost 47–49 to Palmerston North (reckoned the weakest team in the league) they had done enough to win New Zealand's first official league.

Speedway again re-appeared at the 420-yard track at Dunedin so by the time the 1949–50 season drew its curtains there was regular racing at five centres.

The biggest post-war boost to speedway came in 1950 when Ronnie Moore burst on to the British scene. He started at Christchurch in 1948 and spent the months up to 1950 riding in Division Two class meetings at the track.

He was completely unknown in the North Island—until results began filtering through from England where he had joined Wimbledon.

Ronnie became the big name and his British success ensured that speedway began to get coverage on the sports pages of the New Zealand papers.

68

New tracks opened and by March 1950 there was racing at Auckland, Palmerston North, Wellington, Christchurch, Dunedin and Hastings.

In the next couple of seasons Kiwi speedway enjoyed first a boom then a recession. Boom-time saw the first official test matches between England and New Zealand in the 1952–53 season.

Despite the absence of top-liners Ronnie Moore and Trevor Redmond who were racing in South Africa, the home boys clawed their way to a 3–2 test series.

As a matter of New Zealand speedway history the scores and scorers in those first five tests were:

First Test match at Dunedin: New Zealand 36½ (Ron Johnston 16, Geoff Mardon 12½, Maurice Dunn 6, Bob Duckworth 1, Merv Neil 1).

England 35½ (Ken Sharples 17, Chris Boss 7, Bill Kitchen 6½, Eric Williams 4, Jimmy Gooch 1).

Second Test match at Christchurch: New Zealand 31 (Geoff Mardon 12, Merv Neil 10, Maurice Dunn 6, Mick Holland 3).

England 41 (Ken Sharples 12, Chris Boss 15, Eric Williams 9, Bill Kitchen 5).

Third Test Match at Hastings: New Zealand 47 (Ron Johnston 16, Maurice Dunn 12, Peter Clark 10, Geoff Mardon 9).

England 25 (Bill Kitchen 14, Eric Williams 9, Chris Boss 1, Jimmy Gooch 1).

Fourth Test match at Wellington: New Zealand 35 (Maurice Dunn 13, Ron Johnston 12, Geoff Mardon 7, Peter Clark 2, Merv Neil 1).

England 37 (Chris Boss 12, Bill Kitchen 12, Eric Williams 7, Fred Pawson 6).

Fifth Test match at Auckland: New Zealand 47 (Merv Neil 17, Maurice Dunn 13, Ron Johnston 7, Geoff Mardon 7, Peter Clark 3).

England 24 (Eric Williams 10, Terry Small 6, Jimmy Gooch 4, Bill Kitchen 3, Chriss Boss 1).

As far as New Zealand was concerned that—and Ronnie Moore's World Championship success—was the beginning of the establishment in the top grade.

It had taken twenty-five years admittedly. But since then New Zealand has probably taken over as the leading speedway nation in the world although many other countries might dispute this claim.

While we are still searching for the answer to a regular league competition there's racing at nearly a dozen centres in the two Islands—and no country can match our top three.

With ten individual World Speedway titles between them, Ivan Mauger, Barry Briggs and Ronnie Moore have guaranteed the future of speedway in New Zealand.

NEW ZEALAND CHAMPIONSHIP

Year	First	Second	Third
1930	Alf Mattson	Harry Mangham	Eddie Naylor
1931	Alf Mattson	Wally Kilminster	No third
1932–5	Not held		
1936	Wally Kilminster	Not known	Not known
1937–40	Not held		
1941	Charlie Buchanan	Ron Seed	Henry Falls
1942–44	Not held		
1944–5	Jack Hunt	Ron Seed	Norm Morgan
1945–46	Len Perry	Norm Morgan	Goerge Mudgway
1946–47	Gil Craven	Harold Fairhurst	George Mudgway
1947–48	Jack Hunt	Len Perry	Alf Clarkin
1948–49	Harold Fairhurst	Gil Craven	Bruce Abernethy
1949–50	Bruce Abernethy	Trevor Redmond and Alf Clarkin	
1950–51	Bruce Abernethy	Not known	Not known
1951–52	Ron Johnston	Mick Holland	Merv Dunn and Norman Parker
1952–53	Not held		
1953–54	Harold Fairhurst	Merv Neil	Gerald Jackson
1954–55	Not held		
1955–56	Ronnie Moore	Eric Williams	Ron Mountford
1956–57	Not held		
1957–58	Maury Dunn	Julie Benson	Goog Allan
1958–59	Barry Briggs	Ivan Mauger	Len Jelaca
1959–60	Ray New	Maury Dunn	Bryce Subritzky
1960–61	Ray New	Maury Dunn	Bob Anderson
1961–62	Ronnie Moore	Merv Neil	Ken McKinlay
1962–63	Merv Neil	Ronnie Moore	Geoff Mardon
1963–64	Geoff Mardon	Peter Moore	Bob Andrews
1964–65	Murray Burt	Alan Brown	Jack Hart
1965–66	Bob Andrews	Murray Burt	Bryce Subritzky
1966–67	Howard Cole	Doug Templeton	Ronnie Moore
1967–68	Ronnie Moore	Frank Shuter	Bob Andrews
1968–69	Ronnie Moore	Bob Andrews	Goog Allan, Howard Cole and Bill Andrew
1969–70	Chris Bailey	Bill Andrew	Bryce Subritzky
1970–71	Frank Shuter	Alan Brown	Roger Wright
1971–72	Bruce Cribb	Roger Wright	Graeme Stapleton
1972–73	Gary Peterson	Bob Andrews	Graeme Stapleton

BRITISH LEAGUE DIVISION ONE 1973

BELLE VUE, COATBRIDGE, COVENTRY, CRADLEY UNITED, EXETER, HACKNEY WICK, HALIFAX, IPSWICH, KINGS LYNN, LEICESTER, NEWPORT, OXFORD, POOLE, READING, SHEFFIELD, SWINDON, WIMBLEDON, WOLVERHAMPTON.

BRITISH LEAGUE DIVISION TWO 1973

BARROW, BERWICK, BIRMINGHAM, BOSTON, BRADFORD, CANTERBURY, CHESTERTON (STOKE), CREWE, EASTBOURNE, ELLESMERE PORT, HULL, LONG EATON, PETERBOROUGH, RAYLEIGH, SCUNTHORPE, SUNDERLAND, TEES-SIDE, WORKINGTON.

Bath time for Peter Clarke, Maury Dunn, Barry Briggs, Ronnie Moore, Ron Johnston and Jack Cunningham after a New Zealand Championship

Twelve individual titles between them: Ivan Mauger, Barry Briggs and Ronnie Moore

SECOND ☆☆☆ DIVISION STARS

Geoff Bouchard (Long Eaton)   Rod Haynes (Scunthorpe)

Allen Emmett (Rayleigh)

Lou Sansom (Workington)

☆☆☆ SECOND DIVISION STARS

Dave Baugh (Bradford)   Roger Wright (Teesside)

Garry Flood (Crewe)   Richard Greer (Peterborough)

Dennis Wasden (Hull)

THE BLACK SPORT
by Ian MacDonald

Ian MacDonald is recognised as the western world's foremost authority on the sport behind the Iron Curtain.

He is a regular visitor to Eastern Europe and such is his expertise that the Polish Federation have appointed him as their advisor on western speedway.

In this post he advises them on progress outside Poland and is a close friend and confidant of all the top Polish stars.

No-one is better able to trace the history of speedway—a literal translation of the Polish for speedway is 'Black Sport'—behind the Iron Curtain than Ian MacDonald.

'As he came out of the bend he suddenly hit a large bump in the track. Next moment he was draped over the branches of a nearby tree!' Not the opening line of a fiction tale, but one of the many humorous anecdotes eagerly related by an early Polish speedway pioneer.

Polish speedway history is rich in such stories. Some of them, however, are not so funny. Many had tragic consequences. The passing of time has, of course, lent a certain degree of exaggeration, but there is a great deal which is wholly true. In some cases there are even photographs to prove it!

All the stories have one thing in common. They amply illustrate the 'devil-may-care' attitude with which East European speedway is still associated.

The courage of Russian and Polish riders has never been in any doubt. But, often, it has been difficult to decide exactly where 'courage' left off and 'reckless-ness' began! There is no evidence that deliberately dangerous tactics have been used—it's simply an attitude of mind. In speedway, as in nearly everything else, different nations have different characteristics and ideas.

74

The East European tracks are usually longer and wider than their British and Swedish counterparts. They call for an entirely different technique. In Poland and Russia the accent is on speed, speed and more speed. In Britain it is an amalgam of snappy starting and plenty of brainwork which usually takes precedence over sheer speed. The two styles do overlap at times and when a rider has mastered both techniques then, and only then, can he think in terms of becoming World Champion.

The East Europeans, until recently, have tried to ride British tracks in exactly the same way as they would their own. The results have been often disappointing and sometimes disastrous. Major rethinks in policy have been necessary.

Although many of the East European countries engage in regular speedway, it is really only the Poles and Russians who can claim to be in the very front of international activity. Their respective histories differ on many points, but more often than not their 'story' has been closely intertwined. It is a story of two nations, one which climbed slowly to the very top of the speedway tree only to go into gradual decline; whilst the other burst quickly and precociously to the fore—crashed badly—and finally forced its way back. A story of the pupils finally overtaking their teachers and threatening, with justification, to take on the world.

The late Valeri Klementiev (USSR) on the outside of Poland's Piotr Bruzda

The Poles started speedway just after the last war. They were fired with the enthusiasm of British servicemen who had talked in glowing terms about a new sport called 'Dirt-track racing'. They had already heard rumours from their fellow P.O.W's from Czechoslovakia, who had been dabbling with speedway since 1936.

In 1947, the Poles really got down to it. Anyone with a motorbike was to be seen belting around the nearest piece of waste ground—not hard to find in the decimated Polish cities—with head crouched over the handlebars and left leg trailing. The 'tracks' were very crude and one was never quite sure when the guy in front would throw up an unexploded bomb in the path of the other riders as his rear wheel gouged out the dirt. On the face of it, landing in a tree seems a remarkably lucky escape.

Gradually some measure of organisation crept in. A Polish league was formed and, in 1949, the very first Polish Riders' Final was held. The scene of this eagerly awaited event was the Leszno track where the LKM club had been doing business for a little over a year.

Thirteen riders took part—each riding four times. Four points were awarded for a heat win, three for a second, two for a third and one for coming last. This system was used for two seasons.

The first champion was home star Alfred Smoczyk who scored a maximum. Twelve months later, Smoczyk was dead—the victim of a nasty pile-up when defending the trophy at Cracow. Josef Olejniczak, from the Unia Leszno club, went on to complete a maximum, but in an amazing show of emotion, the title was awarded, posthumously, to Smoczyk! Olejniczak is now one of Poland's top trainers and also acts, part-time, as team manager on many of the overseas tours.

In 1951 and 1952 the championship venue was switched to Wroclaw where the old 700 metre track had been replaced by the existing one which has been used for all the major FIM meetings staged by the Poles since 1960. The move to shorten the circuit was the brainchild of Zbigniew Flasinski, a man who has played a major role in organising all the big Wroclaw meetings, including the 1970 world final. Those first two winners at Wroclaw were Wlodzimierz Szwendrowski, from Lublin, in 1951, and Edward Kupczynski, the home skipper, in 1952. Kupczynski was still riding up until the end of the 1970 season.

The 1953 season brought forth a whole host of new riders. One of these, Florian Kapala from Rawicz, shocked the established stars by winning the trophy which, for a change, was run over a series of meetings with aggregate scores counting. Kapala went on to win the title a further three times, including

Ex-Russian Champion Igor Plechanov

Andrzej Wyglenda (Polish Champion 1964/68/69) and (left) Antoni Woryna (Polish Champion 1966)

77

two victories in the colours of a new club, Stal Rzeszow. This is a record which still stands.

Other riders who entered the Polish league at the same time as Kapala included Stanislaw Tkocz, Henryk Zyto, Stefan Kwoczala, Mike Polukard and Marian Kaiser. All of them went on to win the Polish Riders' Final. It was around this bunch that the Poles built their very first Test squad, in 1958.

The team came to Britain that year and were thrashed by three matches to nil. A reciprocal tour was arranged and the British repeated their 3–0 victory. But 1958 was a season very important to the future of the sport. Poland visiting Britain may have been a significant development, but they made one much more sensational decision: they said 'Yes' to an invitation to visit the Soviet Union and train Russian riders!

The Russians had become interested in speedway and were eager to learn all about it. The Poles went to Ufa, a town in the Bashkiriya region, and found a small party of amateur motorcross riders gathered for their very first lesson in the sport they were quickly to dub, 'The Black Sport'.

Three years later, one of these first pupils had qualified for the world final and he went on to become one of speedway's most illustrious stars of the sixties. That rider was—Igor Plechanov!

Ufa became the centre of Russian speedway and the local club side provided most of the riders for the early Test teams which raced in Poland and Czechoslovakia. A league was formed and within a year of that very first 'teach-in' the Russians were holding their first Riders' Championship.

First winner was Ufa's Farid Szajnurov, a rider who hovered around for many seasons without really hitting the big-time. He could never be overlooked, however, and popped-up again in 1966 to win his second championship.

Plechanov established himself as the dominant rider in Russia and won the Russian title in 1960–'61–'63–'65 and 1968. Boris Samorodov, also from Ufa, was champion in 1962 and '64. Samorodov, however, despite a couple of very good world finals, was never consistently up to Plechanov's standard.

While all this early Russian activity was taking place, the Poles were pushed into the background. They hit back in two ways. Firstly, they invited the British back to Poland in 1960, and beat them 2–1. Only brilliant performances by Peter Craven preventing a massacre. The Poles had obviously not been idle. Secondly, they introduced the World Team Cup to the speedway world. It wasn't enough. The Russians still hogged the limelight. Just to make things even worse, the Russians were taking the larger share of Czech speedway bikes which were being exported. The Poles were having to fall back on their own FIS machines which were not in the same class.

The Russians had no such problem and they mounted a fantastic speedway propaganda campaign—aimed at impressing the West. They dismissed invitations to tour Britain and Sweden with the excuse that they were waiting to complete developments on their own super speedway bike. They still travelled around the East European circuits and reports filtered to Britain that the Soviet were winning more matches than they were losing. The Russians fanned the flames by maintaining that their best riders were staying in Russia and weren't on any of the tours.

All this made the British even keener to get the Russians to make a tour. Eventually they arrived—in 1964. There was tremendous advance publicity. Even Fleet Street—usually lethargic in speedway matters in those days—sat up and took the bait. The London-based *Soviet Weekly* magazine enjoyed good sales throughout the tour by virtue of a coloured speedway cover. Ironic really, seeing that speedway results are not printed in any Russian newspapers or periodicals, despite the sport's popularity over there!

Boris Samorodov, Russian Champion 1962 and 1964   *Marian Kaizer, Polish Champion 1957*   *Stanislaw Tkocz, Polish Champion 1958 and 1965*

Unfortunately, the Russians failed to live up to their own publicity—on the track, anyway. Plechanov and Samorodov were great of course, but then we already knew about them. Where were all the mystery superstars? Still in Russia presumably for they certainly weren't on the British tour! Of the 'unknowns' only Gennadi Kurilenko, from the SKA Lvov club, appeared to be up to Test standard.

There were no signs of any super-bikes either. In fact, the ESO machines —with their peculiar foldback handlebars—looked eminently unsuitable for speedway racing.

Despite this, the tour was still a resounding success. The British public were rather hazy about Russia and the Russians. Their only real contact with the Soviets had been in the fifties with the famous Bulganin and Kruschev visit, and a few years later when the first Sputniks hit the headlines of the World's newspapers. Everyone wanted to see these 'mysterious' Russians and a young 'Beatle-mopped' rider from Novosibirsk, called Gabdrakhman Kadirov, became the pin-up boy of the season.

The Russian speedway bubble may have been pricked, but it certainly hadn't burst. The 1964 world final proved that. The Russians took second, fourth and seventh positions through Plechanov, Samorodov and Kurilenko respectively.

However, while the Russians were alternately impressing and baffling us, the Poles were continuing their slow, gradual climb. At Wroclaw, in the European Final of 1964, Zbigniew Podlecki caused a sensation by winning with an untroubled maximum. Doubters were quick to claim that Podlecki was riding on his home track and had trained for two weeks before the final in a muddy field while the top Swedes, like Fundin and Knutsson, had gone to Wroclaw with the sole

Miroslav Verner, Terry Lee and Vaclav Verner (fallen)

purpose of qualifying for the world final. All of which was untrue. Podlecki rode for the Gdansk club—hundreds of miles from Wroclaw—and had been involved in a race for fitness before the final which had kept him away from his bike for several days. Finally, anyone who believes that a 1964 vintage Fundin didn't try to win EVERY race doesn't know his speedway!

Podlecki was a great disappointment in the world final on the rain-soaked Ullevi track—so much for the famous 'muddy field' theory! One Pole who was far from disappointing at Ullevi was Andrzej Wyglenda, from Rybnik, who was a real revelation. Given a dry track, both Podlecki and Wyglenda could have seriously upset the form-book. The unfortunate Podlecki went on to suffer a series of injuries and was eventually paralysed, at the end of the 1972 season, as the result of a road crash. Wyglenda, by contrast, has since won the Polish Riders' Final on three occasions and has also been European and Continental Champion.

These encouraging 1964 performances, by the Poles, turned out to be the mere tip of the proverbial iceberg. This was proved the following season, when the Poles swept to victory in the World Team Cup, in Germany.

In 1966 they improved still further. They trounced the British touring team and retained the World Team Cup. They had opened up a huge gap between themselves and the Russians. They had arrived as a real world force. Another Rybnik rider, Antoni Woryna, finished third in both the European and World Finals. The Russians had only Plechanov. The Poles had Woryna, Pogorzelski, Wyglenda and Waloszek.

The Russians were in grave danger of becoming the forgotten men of international speedway. Kurilenko had failed to make the anticipated step to greatness. Plechanov and Samorodov were losing their sharpness. 1967 Soviet Champion, Viktor Trofimov from Rovno, was too inconsistent, a characteristic of all the new Russians of that era. There were great hopes that Vladimir Smirnov and Anatol Bielkin, two riders from Leningrad, might be different. But it was not to be.

In 1968 the Poles got the chance they had been waiting for; the chance to rub the Soviet nose firmly in the dust. The opportunity came in the World Final at Ullevi. After the scheduled twenty heats had been completed, two riders were tied for third place. They were Poland's Edward Jancarz and Russia's Kurilenko.

Suddenly, this was it. The big confrontation—a test of strength. Like boxers before a big fight, they both received last minute briefings from their respective 'corners'. There was undoubtedly a lot more than a mere World Final third placing at stake. The pre-race 'betting' was about even. Kurilenko had faded as the meeting progressed. Jancarz had got better with each race, but riding with three broken ribs had taken its toll. It was all very intriguing, but the true significance was lost on the majority of the Ullevi crowd.

As it turned out, Jancarz won fairly easily. There was great jubilation in the Polish camp. The Russians slunk away feeling the last nail had been put in their speedway coffin. Ironically, this result was to signal a dramatic and unexpected switch in the fortunes of both nations.

For some reason the Poles began to slide. They began to look a tired speedway team. They just about won the 1969 World Team Cup, at Rybnik, but the warning signals were there. The next season they lost confidence completely. They were staging their very first World Final—but it was too late. Their home advantage had faded. Twelve months later they were humiliated in the World Team Cup on home territory.

The Russians, meanwhile, had changed their policy completely. They actually did unearth new superstars. For a change it wasn't just propaganda. The old brigade disappeared and new riders took over. From the Dynamo Tbilisi club came Valeri Klementiev and Vladek Gordeev. From Novosibirsk came Yuri Dubinin. Klementiev won the 1969 European Final—the first major Soviet success away from East Europe. Dubinin won the Russian Riders' Final and Gordeev the Junior Championship.

In 1970 they consolidated their position. They didn't win anything abroad, but progress was maintained. Gordeev became Soviet Champion—their youngest ever! 1971 looked all set to be a bumper year for them. Instead there was tragedy and disappointment. Klementiev was killed, Dubinin was forced out of speedway for a season with a broken thigh. Gordeev, who almost retired after the death of Klementiev, finished fourth in the World Final, only to be banned from international competition for a year when it was proved he had used an illegal fuel additive.

The Russians showed great character and resolution, and bounced back in 1972. Gordeev was transferred to the **Trud Balakowie** club and became the Soviet Champion for the third year running. In his absence from the international arena, the responsibility of leading the Russian squad was shared by two of the newer stars—Grigori Chlynovski, from Rovno, and Anatol Kuzmin, from Daugavpils.

Gordeev, Chlynovski, Kuzmin: three riders of immense promise. No wonder the Russians are confident of future success.

For the Poles the future is less certain. They have to build again. In Zenon

Plech and Jerzy Szczakiel they have two riders well equipped to take on the rest of the world, but they will have to find that little bit 'extra' which has always eluded their predecessors.

Rest assured that there are plenty of East European thrills and shocks in store during the seventies. Meanwhile, those Polish trees look in remarkably good condition these days—and that can't be bad!

CHAMPIONS

POLAND		RUSSIA	
1949	Alfred Smoczyk		
1950	Alfred Smozcyk		
1951	Wlodzimierz Szwendrowski		
1952	Edward Kupczynski		
1953	Florian Kapala		
1954	Mieczyslaw Polukard		
1955	Wlodzimierz Szwendrowski		
1956	Florian Kapala		
1957	Marian Kaiser		
1958	Stanislaw Tkocz		
1959	Stefan Kwoczala	1959	Farid Szajnurov
1960	Konstanty Pociejkowicz	1960	Igor Plechanov
1961	Florian Kapala	1961	Igor Plechanov
1962	Florian Kapala	1962	Boris Samorodov
1963	Henryk Zyto	1963	Igor Plechanov
1964	Andrzej Wyglenda	1964	Boris Samorodov
1965	Stanislaw Tkocz	1965	Igor Plechanov
1966	Antoni Woryna	1966	Farid Szajnurov
1967	Zygmunt Pytka	1967	Viktor Trofimov
1968	Andrzej Wyglenda	1968	Igor Plechanov
1969	Andrzej Wyglenda	1969	Yuri Dubinin
1970	Edmund Migos	1970	Vladek Gordeev
1971	Jerzy Gryt	1971	Vladek Gordeev
1972	Zenon Plech	1972	Vladek Gordeev

Rod Chessell

Peter White analyses
THE REVIVAL DOWN UNDER

The strength of a country's speedway future lies in the stars it discovers. It is many years since Australian Jack Young stood on the rostrum at Wembley as World Champion in 1952. Since then Australia has been searching for someone to bring the winged wheel back to their country. So far they haven't found anyone although there are many Down Under ready to sing the praises of Jim Airey, John Boulger or Phil Crump.

In this chapter famous Australian writer Peter White tells us something about some of the lesser-known Australian riders. It could be they'll never be heard of again. They may never make international, let alone, world class.

But among them could be a future World Champion. . . .

ROD CHESSELL (Western Australia)
Finished the recent 1972–73 summer season at his home track, Claremont, in Perth, as equal backmarker with veteran star, Chum Taylor, on 140 metres and proved one of the top riders over the season.

From a raw novice in 1969, Chessell capped his short career this season by qualifying for the Australian Championship Final in Sydney. There he scored six points—a creditable performance for an interstate rider having his first-ever outing on the spacious third-of-a-mile Harbour City bowl.

Has a number of placings in big events in Perth to his name, including a third in the 1971–72 City of Perth Championship, second to Ivan Mauger in this year's WA Championship (after brilliantly beating Mauger in one heat) and third to Malcolm Simmons (England) and Chum Taylor in the Governor's Cup.

One of his most memorable meetings is the 1970 WA final of the National Championship.

85

Chessell dropped his bike in the last heat to avoid another rider but re-mounted to finish the race and tie on points for third placing overall. Coura-geously, he won the run-off, riding on instinct alone. The crowd gave him a great ovation as he was assisted to the presentation ceremony and held on the victory dais by the track doctor.

He earned his place in the National Final the hard way . . . but had to withdraw from the meeting to have an operation on his leg.

Now 24, Chessell is on his second visit to Britain where he is currently a member of the Bradford Northern Second Division league team.

BARRY VAN PRAAG (New South Wales)
Barry is the son of the legendary Lionel Van Praag, of Sydney, winner of the first-ever Speedway Championship of the World at Wembley Stadium, London in 1936.

The name has hindered, more than helped, Barry throughout his speedway career and it is only now, after some eight year in the saddle, that 27-year-old Barry is riding out from under his father's shadow.

To emulate a World Champion and a rider who goes into the record books as one of Australia's greatest in the history of the sport is a rather awesome task for any would-be speedway rider and young Barry found it all a bit too much to contend with when his thoughts first turned to racing.

Admittedly, in those seemingly far-off days, the lad was wild, woolly, and, to a degree, somewhat irresponsible astride the snarling speedway steed . . . and he had enough problems simply sorting out the rudiments of the sport without having to worry about proving something as the son of a World Champion.

For a while it looked as if Barry would do little to add glamour to the family name. As a run-of-the-mill novice he struggled and achieved precious little.

Then came a nasty crash at the Kembla Grange speedway, NSW, in which he suffered a very badly smashed foot and ankle. In fact at one stage there were doubts about his ability to walk properly again.

Barry eventually battled his way back from that injury and settled down immediately as a far more mature rider. The 'overnight' transformation was remarkable, and probably a lot of it was to do with confidence.

For his comeback, Barry arranged for Greg Kentwell to send him a brand new British JAP machine from England. Knowing he was now mounted on the best of equipment, it was a do-or-die bid by the boy to prove to all and sundry his own capabilities.

86

Barry Van Praag

Through it all, Barry didn't once lose confidence in himself, in his own ability to make his mark, despite his name.

And so with his newly-found maturity, Barry Van Praag began to progress up the speedway ladder to success. It's been a gradual process . . . slow and steady . . . and this season has seen him emerge as a fully fledged international in the Test match arena and one of the star riders at the Sydney Showground.

Three Test caps were accorded Barry during the summer and a fifth placing in the Australian National Championship Final set the seal on a highly successful stint.

While he may not go on to the World Championship heights of his father, Barry Van Praag has made a name for himself in his own right . . . and one gets the feeling that that in itself is a challenge conquered for this likeable and tenacious star.

Married, and with good career opportunities as a technical engineer in his home town Sydney, Barry has to date resisted offers of a trip to England.

87

GLYN TAYLOR (Western Australia)

According to his Dad, Chum—who is a former World Finalist and should know —18-year-old Glyn is a 'speedway natural'.

'The first time he rode a speedway bike around the track, at Claremont in Perth, he reacted easily and instinctively . . . as if riding the bike was just a natural thing to do,' said veteran campaigner Chum.

'And anyone who has ever tried to race a speedway bike will know just how hard it is to control first time out.'

So it was just one summer season ago Down Under that young Glyn burst on the speedway scene to be hailed as a new find.

Small in stature—just about the right build for a speedway rider—Glyn was branded a stylist right from the beginning and there is little in his current repertoire to suggest there's been any change since his coming to this country . . . as fans at Crewe, where father and son are proving a formidable duo, will readily testify.

This is young Glyn's first racing trip to Britain, although he lays claim to being born in Wales during one of Chum's many competitive sojourns on this side of the world.

Glyn has luckily avoided speedway injuries to date but missed several meetings last Australian season when he suffered a broken bone in a wrist after stepping out of bed one night and tripping over the family dog!

Glyn Taylor . . . a highly capable speedway rider destined for a future possibly even more illustrious than his renowned father.

BARRY FITZGERALD (New South Wales)

A tall, gangling 20-year-old with immense promise in the harsh racket of roaring exhausts and breakneck broadslides of speedway racing—that's Barry Fitzgerald.

Barry hails from the sleepy Sydney suburb of Sefton and has been riding for only a month or two. Already he has made an impressive initial impact and is without doubt the most fiery, tough and most talented of the fifty or so juniors currently embracing the Sydney scene.

Fitzgerald has a heart as large as a mountain when it comes to on-track tenacity . . . but reverts to Mr. Nice Guy once he removes his crash helmet.

He rose from obscurity at provincial tracks to a member of the Sydney Showground First Divison team (for special matches against Newcastle) in a matter of weeks. He suffered a leg injury when he was catapulted head-first into the concrete safety fence at the Showground following a tangle with another competitor, but came back undaunted and is now progressing upwards through the handicap yardage in an endeavour to earn a reputation sufficient to warrant the offer of a trip to England next year.

A close pal of other Sydney youngsters, Wayne Forrest (King's Lynn and Crewe) and Phil Herne (Birmingham), Barry was tempted to join them on their British League baptism this year.

However following an objective look at himself came the realisation that further experience of varying conditions on the different New South Wales bowls such as the Showground, Newcastle, Kembla Grange and Canberra (Tralee) would only serve to enhance his chances of success next year.

So it was a dejected Big Barry Fitzgerald who bade his mates farewell . . . and a rider determined to make his own mark in the very near future.

If nothing else, this lad has a lion-hearted approach to the sport and warrants watching.

Paul Scanlon at Rowley Park

PAUL SCANLON (South Australia)
Paul is a 23-year-old up-and-comer from Adelaide who is on his second visit to England. He is a young man with a varied history that includes an under-16 boxing belt and a skid kid track championship before turning his hand to motorcycles and a spot of sand hill racing at Royal Park (near Adelaide) with Garry Middleton some years ago.

Paul got his break into speedway thanks mainly to former champion rider,

Jock Grierson, and in 1969 he won the Bruce Haythorpe Memorial event at the Renmark speedway, South Australia.

Many placings in major events at Port Pirie and Murray Bridge followed and he progressed to South Australia's premier track—Rowley Park—with plenty of confidence. He impressed immediately with several smart wins from the front mark and was rapidly re-handicapped to 'B' grade status.

He turned out for Sunderland in 1971 for four matches and had the occasional outing at Rye House in an attempt to find his feet in the British League hurly-burly, but returned to Australia soon after rather unobtrusively. However, Paul then proceeded to burn up the Rowley Park track and the summer just concluded ranks as his most impressive season. Paul started from the 170 metre mark and put in some excellent scratch race rides against fierce opposition.

If he can settle he is expected to score well in England.

WAYNE FORREST (New South Wales)
Wayne is one of Sydney's most talented teenagers, and big things are expected from this 19-year-old will o' the wisp.

After the equivalent of one Aussie season in the sport, he headed for England and the League big-time under the Cyril Crane King's Lynn banner.

If he is not pushed too hard, this youngster could very well follow in the tyre tracks of Australia's other illustrious new stars, Phil Crump and Billy Sanders.

Wayne comes a skilled bundle of speedway determination, a mechanically minded motorcyclist who is completely dedicated to reaching the very top of the speedway tree. Last winter in Australia he carried off the season point score competition at the provincial Heddon Greta circuit, north of Sydney, which netted him a handsome $300. He invested the money in a new engine and was rewarded with a booking in the City of Sydney Championship at the Sydney Showground Royale. He performed well and was invited back for subsequent meetings at which he continued to impress.

Wayne hails from the Sydney suburb of Sefton where he is employed as a storeman during the Australian summer. He likes to cross his bike up in power slides which should stand him in good stead on the tight English circuits.

A sure bet for future honours: Wayne Forrest.

STEVE REINKE (Queensland)
A topline Australian international who has resisted all offers of a team contract in favour of the sunnier climes of his native Brisbane. Nevertheless, this 24-year-

old, who is now married, is so talented that it must only be a matter of time before he wilts and tackles the overseas scene.

Steve is an all-round motorcyclist who claimed the Australian scramble, or motocross, championship two years ago. He started speedway at Ipswich and graduated through the ranks to star status at the Brisbane Exhibition Ground —Queensland's premier dirt track venue.

He now has quite a few seasons' experience under his belt . . . which he proved a couple of months ago by annexing the State title (for Queensland) from some very hot opposition which included Halifax rider John Titman, defending champion Jack White and veteran and so-quick stayer, Kevin Torpie.

Steve qualified for the Australian Championship in Adelaide in 1971 and set Rowley Park alight at his first appearance interstate by coming in fourth behind Jim Airey, Ole Olsen and hometown hero John Boulger. He repeated the qualification feat last summer and rode in the National Final in Sydney . . . but finished with a fraction less success following a head-first tumble across Chris Bass when the latter fell on the top shute. He has taken several severe knocks during his career but remains unflurried and is a calm, competent professional who now serves his country with much-appreciated expertise in the Test match arena.

Steve really takes some beating around his home track, the Brisbane Exhibition Ground, and can go on to bigger things yet.

Geoff Snider

DON HOWISON (New South Wales)

Don is a little-known character from the New South Wales coalfields area around Cossnock/Newcastle, the breeding ground for so much speedway talent of the past including such legendaries as leg trailing heroes Billy Lamont and Tommy Benstead and present day First Division Tiger, Bob Valentine, of Sheffield.

In fact it was in the lush Hunter Valley area that speedway first had its beginnings—under the astute guidance of Johnnie Hoskins back in the 1920s. That's another story, however, and one that doesn't concern our Don.

The lad with the mop of hair has emerged as Newcastle's most likely international prospect for some years and is attached to Second Division league track Barrow in England.

He's taken a bold step by travelling overseas after only a matter of months in the sport but if anyone can make it pay dividends, it's Don.

An extremely amiable and pleasant type, Don shows a lot of latent motorcycle ability and is a product of the short circuits (akin to English grass tracks) in the north of New South Wales. He started his speedway at the Sydney Showground and continually top scored for the Newcastle Second Division side in team matches shortly before his departure from these shores.

A rapid-improver, Don looks likely to go from strength to strength and lucky could be the promoter who has picked up the option on this hitherto 'unknown'.

GEOFF SNIDER (South Australia)

A 19-year-old butcher from Adelaide, Geoff is single and just itching to take a crack at the British League—and 1974 will be his year if all goes according to plan.

His elder brother, Ray, started riding in 1968 and when young Geoff nipped around for a trial on big brother's bike he was so impressive that he was persuaded to enter the sport himself. He bought an ex-Charlie Monk/Bryan Elliott-ridden machine last season and had one ride . . . fell off . . . and packed it in! Fortunately the latter state of affairs was only temporary and he returned for a serious assault during the last Australian summer season.

Turned out in red, white and blue leathers, Geoff got it all together and put in some good performances, despite a hectic style. He has received a lot of tuition from Bill Amundson and is currently in the throes of purchasing a new machine for the 1973–74 Aussie season.

With his sights set firmly on that long-awaited trip to England next term, Geoff Snider should figure prominently on the Adelaide scene from here on.

Peter Oakes introduces those SCANDINAVIAN SUPERSTARS

Soren Sjosten

Several years ago there was a concerted move to ban all Swedish riders from the British League.

Indeed, for one season such a ban was in force.

It wasn't long though before the crowds demanded the re-appearance of the Scandinavian wonder-boys. And was it any wonder?

British speedway would be a lot poorer for their absence as some of the photographs in the following pages will show.

For a long time Swedish speedway dominated the world rankings as Ove Fundin proved himself a world champion without equal, with a succession of final night extravanganzas that culminated in five world titles going to the Tranas wonder.

At one time it looked as if Fundin was to find a rival from his own doorstep when Southampton's prized capture Bjorn Knutsson joined the immortal few who could add World Speedway Champion to his name in 1965.

The Bear, unfortunately, had had enough of speedway glamour and retired from the shale tracks at the time when his earnings should have been at their peak.

Undoubtedly the sorry state of National League speedway in build-up days accounted for Knutsson's surprising exit from international speedway and had he won the title in the far richer days since the formation of the British League he might still be around today.

93

Certainly his contemporary Barry Briggs—they were one-time team-mates at Southampton forming what must rank as the deadliest of all spearheads—is capable of winning races with gay abandon today.

But Knutsson wasn't content to bathe in the non-materialistic glory of his speedway fame in those days. Instead he decided he would concentrate on the more lucrative Continental long-track market.

By doing that he probably earned money faster and easier than if he had remained in speedway, but at the same time he robbed the sport of his glory days.

Since Knutsson—and ignoring the peerless Fundin who's reign started some years earlier—Sweden hasn't produced another World Champion. Bernt Persson was four laps away from glory last year but it was Bengt Jansson who came closest of all in 1967 when he lost a debatable run-off with Fundin at Wembley.

Former Swedish World Champion Bjorn Knutsson

Ever popular Bengt Jansson

Stories about that night are plentiful and there are many informed commentators—both sides of the fence—who still believe that the title should have gone to Jansson.

Many believed then that the Swedish officials were happy to see Fundin win; and confident that Jansson's promotion to the throne was being delayed for only a year.

Instead Jansson's grip on the trophy slackened and until he surged into third place in the controversial 1971 Gothenburg final, he hasn't figured on the rostrum.

Soren Sjosten—the battler from Folkarna—slipped into the third place in 1969 and managed fourth a year later but other than that Sweden's cup had not exactly run over with success . . . until Persson's glory night at Wembley last year.

That aside they have laid claim to being the speedway nation of the sixties. A title that has slipped from their grasp with alarming speed since the birth of the seventies.

But there is still no-one who disputes that the Swedish riders are a welcome, if expensive, addition to the British speedway scene.

Forking out upwards of £1,000 a season on trans-North Sea crossings is no happy way to spend the profits but promoters realise that so many of the Swedes are the men who make the turnstiles clatter.

Admittedly a few small fish have slipped through the net and found themselves completely overawed in the big pond but any list of today's most attractive riders must include a fair smattering of Scandinavians.

Olle Nygren was the man who started it all back in 1949 when as a blond wonder-boy he wowed the fans down on the South Coast when skippering a Swedish side making its first British tour.

Since then Olle has been more or less a permanent member of the establishment and having married an English girl probably sees himself more British than Swedish.

Certainly, unlike some of his fellow countrymen, he spends more time in his adopted homeland than in Sweden.

Now embarked on another new career leading Ipswich's Division One assault there are still many years of active points-gathering in the ample frame of Mr. Nygren.

Olle has been here so long that anyone else seems a comparative newcomer. But there are some who have been here quite a few years.

Soren Sjosten, one of the smallest riders in the game and certainly one of the bounciest, joined Belle Vue back in 1963. He's had one of two spells out of the game but now he's another Anglicised Swede having married a Manchester butcher's daughter and developed a somewhat un-nerving Mancunian accent to his native Nordic tongue.

Bengt Jansson hasn't married English but he, too, has been accepted as 'one of us.' A career that began at Edinburgh and took him to West Ham blossomed when he became leader of the Hackney Hawks—in spirit if not name—and his last lap dashes round the outside make him a firm favourite wherever he rides.

Youthful enthusiasm is an ingrown asset in the Swedish make-up and 19-year-old Tommy Johansson showed it in plenty during his first visit heading the Young Sweden test team in 1970.

So much so that he was immediately signed by Newport and proved a bargain first-year student the following year. He kept it up at Ipswich until a blood disorder ruled him out of regular British League racing.

Good-looking Anders Michanek—one-time pin up boy of the Midlands and now flooring them at Reading—never really lived up to the immense promise he displayed when he first joined Long Eaton in 1967 until this year and now on his day he can beat anyone in the world . . . and that means anyone.

Luck—or is it true world-class ability?—always seems to have deserted him when a World Champion medal has hung on the end of the meeting.

Like Michanek, Gote Nordin is good-looking and an all-time favourite with the fans. His reputation as a true ambassador of sport has remained unimpaired throughout his career and a third place in the 1961 World final has been scant reward for a career that has always scaled the heights.

Nordin, whose visits to Britain have been few and far between in recent seasons, is one of the old school and a stylist to boot.

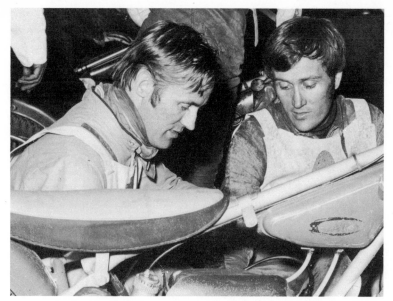

Gote Nordin chats to Anders Michanek between races

Bernt Persson

While others may thrill the fans with their wild and seemingly uncontrolled broadsides across the searing shale, Nordin is a man who never seems troubled.

His armchair style of riding may not please those who want their speedway with spectacle but it is pure honey to the true afficionado.

That Nordin has never won a world title is one of those incongruities that will never be explained. At international and international individual level he has proved his worth time and time again but never when the ultimate prize has been at stake.

It could fairly be said that Fundin, Nygren, Nordin, Sjosten, Jansson and Michanek belong to the old school of Swedish rider although by that there is no inference that they are past their best.

It is just that they have been around longer than some of the new-breed Swedes.

One of these is blond Christer Lofqvist now enjoying life among the Bournemouth Belles and the harbour breezes of Dorset. On the demise of West Ham he was swiftly switched to Poole where his all-action style has gone down well.

To liken Lofqvist to anyone else is fanciful but if one is to describe his style in anything like an accurate form he is a combination of the late Peter Craven, Soren Sjosten and Torbjorn Harryson.

What he lacks that the other three all had is the consistency to make his style pay-off among superior opposition. But then Lofqvist is still a young man and has none of the experience of the other three.

It was Harryson who probably held more Swedish hopes than anyone else of lifting a World title. He was sensational on his final debut in 1968 and a real danger when it was held at Wembley a year later.

A first bend clash with a couple of riders ended with Harryson being carted off to a Middlesex Hospital with a broken thigh and since then he has put on weight and struggled to make an abortive come-back.

Whether doctors will ever allow Toby to recapture the form that made him the toast of Wales some years ago remains to be seen.

If Czechoslovakia's Jiri Stancl was the shock man of the Eastern bloc contingent in the 1971 World Final then Tommy Jansson—no relation to Bengt—was the European equivalent.

Wembley had dispensed with his services after a handful of meetings as he showed no real sign of adapting to the British tracks. He went back home and instead of brooding taught everyone a lesson.

Outclassed though he was at Gothenburg the young Jansson gave notice that he is going to take a leading part in the fortunes of Swedish speedway in the years to come as his form with Wimbledon these past two seasons has shown.

Swedes don't monopolise the commodity of excitement however and there have been many disappointments as British promoters have searched for the young fireball they need to pull in the extra fans.

Bernie Persson, now happily esconsced in the Midlands after an exciting start in Scotland, was one of those who provided the goods.

Others haven't done so well—particularly in Scotland.

Bo Josefsson had a couple of years in Glasgow's colours without proving anything more than a higher than average second string below-average heat leader. Nils Ringstrom didn't even achieve that.

Bengt Larsson has never really adequately bridged the gap between second string and heat leader despite several seasons at Sheffield and kronor millionaire Bengt Brannefors has always flattered to deceive.

At times brilliant, something has always held him back and now it is unlikely that he will ever settle down to a permanent British League berth.

Hasse Holmkvist, the lantern-jawed racer from Stockholm, has provided plenty of points in a career of high drama and low farce but a series of domestic troubles has retarded his natural progression.

Of the younger brigade, Poole promoter Mr. Charles Foote still has more than high hopes that Bo Wirebrand will join the select band of Swedish super-stars and forecast that he will be there or thereabouts within the next two seasons.

At Poole Wirebrand—who first came to Poole's attention with an impressive display when Britain visited Sweden for a test series two winters ago—has suffered from a lack of consistency but once or twice shown flashes of sheer brilliance.

It could be that out of all the 'wonder-boys' on display today that it is Wirebrand who proves the best of them all.

Tommy Jansson slings it down

STAR ✪✪✪✪
SPANGLED
BANNER ✪

One of the speedway success stories of recent years has been the re-emergence of American speedway.

Long before the Second World War the Yanks held sway and provided two competitors in the first ever World Speedway Championship Final back in 1936.

A season later Jack Milne, now a Californian businessman and one of the leading lights in the speedway revival back in the States, picked up a 15-point maximum to become the 1937 World Champion—with brother Cordy slotted neatly into third place: the first and only time two brothers have shared the world final tractor ride.

Again in 1938 the American challenge was prominent with holder Milne failing to retain his title by a solitary point. And again it was an American who filled the third place . . . this time being Wimbledon recruit Wilbur Lamoreaux, who had been runner-up the previous season.

Speedway boomed States-side and a handful of their top racers added colour, spectacle and skill to British speedway at places like New Cross, Bristol, Harringay and West Ham.

Indeed, but for the war there could again have been an American clean sweep on the 1939 championship as a fourth countryman—Southampton's Benny Kaufman—reached the final sixteen only to see his hopes of a World Final debut blown to bits by Hitler.

Once the war was over speedway was revived both sides of the Atlantic and Lamoreaux managed to span the ten-season gap by reading his fourth successive world final

He'd finished second in 1937, third a year later: but the war had taken too much out of him and he dropped a further two places to finish fifth behind the fourth Englishman.

America's challenge was over, although a couple of seasons later Ernie Roccio was to reach his sole World Final although he struggled at the foot of the field.

A year or so later he was to be killed on the track . . . and with his death passed any American hopes of re-asserting their former influence on the world's greatest individual title.

Since then several Americans have tried to break into British speedway with little success. Don Hawley and his Californian buddies tried it in the fifties.

DeWayne Keeter tried it at Leicester in the late sixties.

But no-one made it—until this year when three Americans—blond Scott Autrey, a 19-year-old from Bellflower, California; National Champion Rick Woods from Costa Mesa, California; and wealthy Sumner McKnight, a New Yorker with roots in the Western States—decided to throw up their comfortable and easy American style-of-life for the rugged life-style of British League racing.

Woods joined Newport . . . Autrey went to Exeter . . . and McKnight linked with Swindon.

The way the Americans are used to seeing Sumner McKnight, pulling hard at the Costa Mesa

Unhappily for them they weren't able to revive the palmy days of the Milne Brothers in the World Championship—in fact they weren't even allowed to compete in the British qualifying rounds because of their American heritage.

But they did prove one thing: American speedway is near ready to take its place in the world of international sport.

League racing—between Californian tracks Costa Mesa, Bakersfield, Irwindale and Ventura—brought English-style competition to the States but it didn't catch on with the crowds on the benches and within a few months promoters switched back to the popular programme format of scratch and handicap races.

With up to six riders a time on tracks barely an eighth of a mile long, racing can be wild and hairy. Through the cameras of ace American photographers Dennis Greene and Ralph Currier we now bring speedway American-style into your living-room!

Harry Oxley's star-studded side at Costa Mesa: (l. to r.) US Champion Rick Woods, Ex-Champ Steve Bast, Don Cullum, Greg Haserot, Ron Stewart, Larry Moon and John Fishburn, with Harry Oxley (bottom right)

A large wire fence does not deter girl fans who want Scott Autrey's autograph

American style of speedway as illustrated by top-ranking Larry Shaw

Former World Speedway Champion Jack Milne at the 1972 American Awards Banquet

PICTURE FLASHBACK

Flashback to the Thirties—and speedway at Monica Park, Christchurch, New Zealand. Lined up left to right are: Jack Hobson, Eric Langton, Bill Ferguson, Bill Dumpleton, Art Lamport, Marty Rush, Rewi Dickson, Dicky Case, Lionel Van Praag (World Champion in 1936) Norman Neil and Charlie Saunders

1935—and Dicky Case, Lionel Van Praag, Jack Hobson and Wally Kilminster prepare for a vital race

A team that died: Southampton, 1963. Left to right: Brian Clements, Bjorn Knutsson, Barry Briggs, Peter Vandenberg, Cyril Roger, Alby Golden, Reg Luckhurst, Captain Dick Bradley on bike

Fifteen years old—and Ivan Mauger is ready to take on the world

The Stoke team that competed in the provincial league: Left to right: Ron Sharpe, Peter Morrish, Ken Adams, Ray Harris (on bike), Colin Pratt, Bill Wainwright, Peter Jarman and John Edwards

THE TWIN TOWERS OF MAGIC | by Peter Oakes

They call it the greatest stadium in the world.

Architecturally it may not be everything. But ask any sportsman to name the greatest stadium in the world and he'll plump for that monastic looking, twin-towered edifice at the foot of Empire Way.

Wembley. The home of English international soccer. Wembley. The mecca for the annual pilgrims from North Country rugby league centres. Wembley. The scene of the screaming mass of jolly-hockey-stick schoolgirls. Wembley. Venue of the all-Irish Hurling Final.

You name any sport and the odds are that it has been staged by the Sir Arthur Elvin-built emporium at some time or another.

Speedway? Now there's a subject that goes down well at Wembley. Dating back to 1929 when Wembley became founder members of the Southern League.

Since then the bikes have roared round the red-shale circuit at the Empire Stadium on and off for 43 years.

There was a lull in activity throughout the last three years of the fifties and the entire sixties but speedway was re-born at the Middlesex stadium three years ago.

Then millionaire Bernard Cottrell—whose multi-storey office block virtually overlooks the mighty royal box stand at Wembley—joined forces with his one-time idol Trevor Redmond to bring league racing back to its original home.

Every year Wembley had opened its massive double pit gates for a speedway classic—a World Final; a World Team Cup Final; or merely a European Final —but no-one dreamt that it could become a weekly league track.

Many scoffed at Cottrell's temerity in believing he could revive the glory-glory days of the middle fifties when the roaring Lions devoured all opposition.

But that wasn't Cottrell's plan. He didn't want to devastate. He wanted to consolidate. And above all bring his beloved speedway back to the place he always felt it belonged.

It would be churlish to pretend that he succeeded one hundred per cent.

Admittedly he brought a new public dimension to the sport with brave, bright ideas on presentations and showmanship. A lion cub preceded the pre-match parade on opening night.

Bob Danvers-Walker—the man famous for the gong in Hughie Green's now re-named *Double Your Money*—and children's favourite Ed 'Stewpot' Stewart were booked as co-announcers for the first season.

Stewart proved a great favourite while Danvers-Walker faded from the scene. Another television star—David Hamilton, more used to working at the Wembley studios than the Wembley stadium—helped out and big-time sponsors made sure that Wembley was never short of publicity.

Ivan Mauger and Bernie Persson at the Wembley Gate . . . before the run-off that decided the 1972 World Final

A confined first season—cut short by conflicting sports attractions—did little to deter the Wembley regulars and while crowds never threatened to climb up to the eldorado days of a regular 50,000 the support did match that of any other team in the country.

The familiar red and white body colours were seen once again and the Lions started to build up a pretty useful side that provided nothing if not attractive opposition everywhere they rode.

In that first season the basis of the side was centred around the Coatbridge line-up and included Scots Bert Harkins and Brian Collins and domiciled Scots Wayne Briggs (a New Zealander by birth) and Norwegian champion Reidar Eide. With Tim Bungay also a fairly regular member of the septet the Lions established a reasonable home record but were disappointing on their travels.

Fleeting appearances from five-times World champion Ove Fundin, bespectacled Swede Bengt Andersson, American Steve Best and another nine or so riders didn't help matters too much.

The Lions did, however, make two signings, one that was to have an important bearing on the following season's showing.

Signing number one was Brian Leonard from Newport. And number two: 18-year-old Dave Jessup who became the first Second Division rider to be transferred to a Division One side other than through his parent track.

Jessup made enough impact in 1970 to show he was capable of rising to great heights and how Wembley must have wished they had signed him three months earlier.

Winter boardroom discontent led to a somewhat new look Wembley lining up for the 1971 season. Director Bernard Cottrell withdrew from day-to-day running of the team and at one time resigned his directorship although retaining his shares in the company.

This left Trevor Redmond holding the reins and he immediately began the task of strengthening his side. Reidar Eide moved on to Poole. Tim Bungay was to retire. Wayne Briggs went to Exeter. And Ove Fundin prematurely called it a day.

Harkins, Jessup, Collins and Leonard remained (as did Bungay for a week or so) and Wembley fortified their line-up with the signing of Tony Clarke (an English international of considerable experience); Sverre Harrfeldt (probably Norway's leading rider whose career had been threatened following a disastrous European Final injury sustained in Poland) and former Swedish World Finalist Hasse Holmkvist.

With that sort of talent parade they could have been expected to top the league. Instead Holmkvist decided to stay at home and Clarke hit the sort of spell when nothing would go right.

All-time favourite Gote Nordin—probably Sweden's most popular stylist —agreed to help out for a couple of months but his absence was sorely felt when he returned home, as he had indicated all along, to continue studies.

Tommy Jansson was discarded and went on to show how wrong Wembley were by reaching the World Final; and Christer Sjosten was no Soren.

Despite all this the Lions finished in a comfortable mid-table position and retained their reputation as one of the Division's big crowd-pullers.

With two testing seasons behind them promoters Trevor Redmond and Bernard Cottrell embarked on the following season with a promise of rich glories.

Still missing that vital third heat leader of international repute to back up the steadily-improving and volatile Bert Harkins and the enigmatic Cockney Tony Clarke, the Wembley management held a series of mid-winter conferences.

The outcome was a decision to allow unsettled Dave Jessup—the 1970 Divison Two Riders Champion—to move.

In his place they were given the 1968 Division Two Riders Champion . . . fiery Midlander Graham Plant.

Gote Nordin helped Wembley out— and has been a regular visitor to the Wembley track for individual and team events

Brave Sverre Harrfeldt recovered from a serious injury to show some of his old form in Wembley's colours

Unhappy in his role as number three at Leicester—overshadowed by England's top pointsman Ray Wilson and Australian Champion John Boulger —Plant jumped at the chance of the move and saw his opportunity to stake a claim to a regular place in the English international squad.

It was with this enhanced line-up that the 1972 Wembley Lions began preparations for their third season in the British League.

A season that was to hold out such promise. A season in which their administrators genuinely considered they were in with a championship chance.

Then one dismal Thursday morning in February—at the height of the miners' strike power crisis—came the Wembley blackout.

THERE WOULD BE NO REGULAR LEAGUE SPEEDWAY AT THE EMPIRE STADIUM IN 1972.

The bombshell echoed throughout the country as all the national papers carried stories of the downfall of the mighty Lions.

Officially the Wembley management said there could be no weekly speedway because of conflicting fixtures at the stadium. Association football went far into June with the European Nations Cup and an earlier than usual international beginning at the other end of the season would not give Wembley their eighteen

Bert 'Haggis' Harkins. From a reliable points-scorer in Scotland he became an extrovert showman in Middlesex

Now with Poole, Brian Collins moved south for Wembley's final league season

essential league dates.

So the re-birth was cut off in infancy. Trevor Redmond nursed hopes that he could transplant his baby to Cornish resort St. Austell—a former Provincial League base where TR maintained stock car rights—but that move was defeated on several grounds: not least because of the track's far-away inaccessibility.

The Wembley team was broken up. Tony Clarke went to Newport. Brian Collins to Poole. Graham Plant to Newport. And so on. . . .

Even now there are hopes that Wembley will re-appear in the league fixtures. Certainly the stadium isn't completely lost to the sport.

But will the Lions roar again at Empire Stadium? Who can say?

It is, and always has been, the number one choice to stage the World Speedway Championship Final and this year the Wembley authorities also agreed to allow the track to be used for the climax of the newly-launched *Daily Mirror-*sponsored World League.

And as long as there's still a speedway track at the Empire Stadium there must always be the hope that someone—perhaps Trevor Redmond, perhaps somebody else—will bring league racing back to the twin towers of magic. . . .

Today Wembley is synonymous with the World Final—and bubbly

ACTION ALL THE WAY

It's action all the way . . . whether it's Rayleigh or Wroclaw. Leningrad or Costa Mesa. Ruhpolding or Sydney.

On these pages we bring you action the world over—with some exclusive shots from behind the Iron Curtain.

Right: A typical action shot of the Poles in action— Jan Mucha (left), Stanislaw Bombik (centre) and Andrzej Wyglenda

Exeter's Kevin Holden lets her fly!

American Rick Woods in big, big trouble

*Left: Division Two
action from (l. to r.)
Bob Young, Tiger
Beech, Ross Gilbertson
and Ted Hubbard*

*Right: Three nations
action in the 1968
European Final—
(l. to r.) Pawel
Waloszek (Poland),
Martin Ashby
(England) and
Vladimir Smirnov
(U.S.S.R.)*

*Left: American team
racing at Costa Mesa—
(l. to r.) Ed Williams,
Rick Woods, Dan Becker
and John Fishburn*

WHAT'S THIS THEN?

Ivan Mauger switches to sidecar racing!

It gets a bit hot in Australia! Phil Crump hoses down
Ivan Mauger

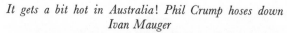

Above: Ivan at the Houston Astro-
dome, U.S.A., riding a 250 c.c.
Kawasaki in American Class 'C'
racing

The British League 1965~1972

BRITISH LEAGUE 1965

WEST HAM	...	...	...	34	16	0	1	781	542	7	1	9	649	673	47
WIMBLEDON	...	...	...	34	15	1	1	767	553	7	1	9	629	692	46
COVENTRY	...	...	...	34	16	0	1	769	549	4	0	13	615	709	40
OXFORD	...	...	...	34	14	0	3	717	607	5	2	10	591	733	40
HALIFAX	...	...	...	33	13	3	1	754	564	5	0	11	568	676	39
NEWPORT	...	...	...	34	17	0	0	802	523	2	0	15	558	765	38
WOLVERHAMPTON	...	...	34	15	1	1	819	506	3	0	14	610	710	37
HACKNEY WICK	...	...	34	16	0	1	783½	537½	2	1	14	544	782	37
EXETER	...	...	...	34	16	0	1	787	539	2	0	15	538½	784½	36
POOLE	...	...	...	34	14	0	3	780	540	3	1	13	598	726	35
SHEFFIELD	...	...	...	34	14	1	2	761	564	2	1	14	539	782	34
NEWCASTLE	...	...	...	34	14	1	2	782	543	2	0	15	581	739	33
GLASGOW	...	...	...	34	13	0	4	784	540	2	1	14	531	789	31
BELLE VUE	...	...	...	34	15	0	2	792	532	0	0	17	536	780	30
SWINDON	...	...	...	34	12	1	4	744	577	1	1	15	601	723	28
CRADLEY HEATH	...	...	33	10	1	5	621	626	1	0	16	511	812	23
EDINBURGH	...	...	...	34	11	0	6	680	641	0	0	17	493	830	22
LONG EATON	...	...	...	34	5	0	12	631	685	2	0	15	574	849	14

(NB: Fixture Cradley Heath v. Halifax was rained-off and never run)

BRITISH LEAGUE 1966

HALIFAX	...	...	...	36	17	0	1	877	527	10	0	8	697	702	54
COVENTRY	...	...	...	36	18	0	0	866	537	7	1	10	682	718	51
SWINDON	...	...	...	36	18	0	0	891	509	5	0	13	662	730	46
WIMBLEDON	...	...	...	36	17	0	1	835	566	5	0	13	650	748	44
NEWCASTLE	...	...	...	36	17	0	1	857½	541½	3	0	15	634	763	40
POOLE	...	...	...	36	16	0	2	822½	576½	3	2	13	620½	779½	40
WEST HAM	...	...	...	36	15	0	3	830	573	4	1	13	669½	731½	39
GLASGOW	...	...	...	36	17	0	1	819	567	1	0	17	576	827	36
WOLVERHAMPTON	...	...	36	16	0	2	773	626	1	2	15	567½	835½	36
EXETER	...	...	...	36	15	1	2	810	589	2	0	16	582½	814½	35
SHEFFIELD	...	...	...	36	17	0	1	848	555	0	0	18	562	839	34
EDINBURGH	...	...	...	35	16	0	2	796½	605½	1	0	16	514	808	34
BELLE VUE	...	...	...	36	16	0	2	817	586	0	0	18	545	857	32
HACKNEY WICK	...	...	36	14	1	3	759½	643½	1	0	17	588	813	31
OXFORD	...	...	...	36	13	2	3	743	656	1	0	17	548	854	30
KINGS LYNN	...	...	...	36	14	0	4	746	652	1	0	17	529	872	30
NEWPORT	...	...	...	36	12	1	5	774	630	0	0	18	545	856	25
LONG EATON	...	...	...	36	12	1	5	750	648	0	0	18	536	868	25
CRADLEY HEATH	...	...	35	10	0	7	659	657	0	0	18	537	849	20

NB: Fixture Cradley Heath v. Edinburgh was rained-off and never run)

BRITISH LEAGUE 1967

SWINDON	...	...	...	36	18	0	0	887	514	6	0	12	649	752	48
COVENTRY	...	...	...	36	17	0	1	882	517	5	2	11	642	758	46
WEST HAM	...	...	...	36	17	0	1	862	540	4	3	11	652	748	45
EDINBURGH	...	...	...	36	16	1	1	861	540	4	1	13	624	778	42
HACKNEY WICK	...	...	...	36	17	1	0	824	578	3	0	15	578	822	41
POOLE	...	...	...	36	16	1	1	829	572	1	2	15	633	767	37
HALIFAX	...	...	...	36	16	1	1	857	545	2	0	16	599	804	37
WOLVERHAMPTON	...	...	...	36	17	0	1	824	573	1	1	16	599	803	37
SHEFFIELD	...	...	...	36	16	1	1	795½	604½	2	0	16	538	866	37
NEWCASTLE	...	...	...	36	16	0	2	807	595	2	0	16	579	822	36
WIMBLEDON	...	...	...	36	15	1	2	775	623	1	2	15	617	786	35
NEWPORT	...	...	...	36	14	1	3	819	584	3	0	15	568	829	35
GLASGOW	...	...	...	36	13	1	4	771	628	3	1	14	572	829	34
OXFORD	...	...	...	36	15	1	2	810½	591½	1	0	17	558	841	33
EXETER	...	...	...	36	16	0	2	843	560	0	0	18	541½	858½	32
BELLE VUE	...	...	...	36	14	0	4	756	643	2	0	16	577½	820½	32
LONG EATON	...	...	...	36	13	3	2	749	654	1	0	17	573	827	31
CRADLEY HEATH	...	...	...	36	11	0	7	739	658	1	0	17	523	875	24
KINGS LYNN	...	...	...	36	11	0	7	759	641	0	0	18	537	864	22

BRITISH LEAGUE DIVISION ONE 1968

COVENTRY	...	...	...	36	17	0	1	825	578	5	0	13	611	791	44
HACKNEY WICK	...	...	...	36	18	0	0	801	600	3	2	13	620	783	44
EXETER	...	...	...	36	18	0	0	927	474	2	1	15	629½	774½	41
SHEFFIELD	...	...	...	36	18	0	0	866½	536½	2	1	15	597	801	41
NEWCASTLE	...	...	...	36	18	0	0	837	566	2	0	16	617	784	40
WEST HAM	...	...	...	36	16	0	2	794	604	3	1	14	660	744	39
HALIFAX	...	...	...	36	17	1	0	846	557	2	0	16	578	822	39
COATBRIDGE	...	...	...	36	16	1	1	838	563	2	0	16	566	834	37
WIMBLEDON	...	...	...	36	17	0	1	837	562	1	0	17	574	822	36
BELLE VUE	...	...	...	36	16	0	2	819	585	2	0	16	568	832	36
SWINDON	...	...	...	36	14	0	4	839	560	3	1	14	609	793	35
LEICESTER	...	...	...	36	16	1	1	770	631	1	0	17	603	799	35
NEWPORT	...	...	...	36	17	1	0	823	579	0	0	18	525	878	35
CRADLEY HEATH	...	...	...	36	13	1	4	783	620	2	3	13	590	810	34
OXFORD	...	...	...	36	16	0	2	774	628	1	0	17	545	859	34
WOLVERHAMPTON	...	...	...	36	16	0	2	800	600	0	0	18	588	813	32
POOLE	...	...	...	36	13	2	3	755	658	0	0	18	572	830	28
KINGS LYNN	...	...	...	36	13	1	4	763	636	0	0	18	567	837	27
GLASGOW	...	...	...	36	11	1	6	757	647	2	0	16	555	848	27

BRITISH LEAGUE DIVISION TWO 1968

BELLE VUE II	...	...	...	18	9	0	0	464	236	5	0	4	348	346	28
NELSON	...	...	...	18	9	0	0	426	271	2	0	7	309	391	22
MIDDLESBROUGH	...	...	...	18	8	0	1	399	299	2	1	6	312	388	21
PLYMOUTH	...	...	...	18	9	0	0	421	280	1	0	8	283	413	20
RAYLEIGH	...	...	...	18	8	0	1	399	294	1	1	7	301	397	19
CRAYFORD	...	...	...	18	8	0	1	435	260	0	1	8	278	420	17
CANTERBURY	...	...	...	18	7	1	1	377	322	1	0	8	268	432	17
READING	...	...	...	18	6	1	2	388	313	0	1	8	287	412	14
WEYMOUTH	...	...	...	18	5	2	2	379	319	0	0	9	275	421	12
BERWICK	...	...	...	18	5	1	4	367	328	0	0	9	261	435	10

BRITISH LEAGUE DIVISON ONE 1969

POOLE	...	...	...	36	18	0	0	850½	550½	8	1	9	668	734	53
BELLE VUE	...	...	...	36	18	0	0	865	536	5	1	12	668	732	47
WIMBLEDON	...	...	...	36	18	0	0	908½	483½	4	2	12	647	755	46
HALIFAX	...	...	...	36	18	0	0	889	515	4	2	12	594	729	46
LEICESTER	...	...	...	36	16	0	2	833	570	5	2	11	660	742	44
SHEFFIELD	...		...	36	18	0	0	848	554	1	1	16	619½	782½	39
CRADLEY HEATH	...		...	36	16	1	1	778	621	2	1	15	598	805	38
GLASGOW	...	...	...	36	15	2	1	818	583	2	1	15	605	797	37
KINGS LYNN	...	...	...	36	16	0	2	799	601	2	0	16	614	789	36
SWINDON	...	...	...	36	15	0	3	770	627	3	0	15	621	781	36
COATBRIDGE	...	...	...	36	15	1	2	788	616	2	0	16	602	802	35
EXETER	...	...	...	36	15	0	3	789	612	1	0	17	588	814	32
NEWCASTLE	...	...	...	36	14	1	3	783	615	1	1	16	565	835	32
COVENTRY	...	...	...	36	13	3	2	709	603	1	0	17	620½	780½	31
OXFORD	...	...	...	36	13	1	4	754	571	2	0	16	536	865	31
WOLVERHAMPTON	...	...	...	36	12	0	6	739	664	1	1	16	572	830	27
NEWPORT	...	...	...	36	13	1	4	760	641	0	0	18	496	905	27
WEST HAM	...	...	...	36	10	2	6	711	693	1	1	16	565	834	25
HACKNEY WICK	...	...	...	36	10	2	6	720	682	0	0	18	510	890	22

BRITISH LEAGUE DIVISION TWO 1969

BELLE VUE II	...	...	...	30	14	0	1	785	380	9	1	5	609	558	47
READING	...	...	...	30	13	1	1	678	481	6	0	9	543	622	39
ROMFORD	...	...	...	30	11	0	4	649	517	8	1	6	573	592	39
CRAYFORD	...	...	...	30	15	0	0	730	434	4	0	11	544½	621½	38
RAYLEIGH	...	...	...	30	12	1	2	671	495	4	1	10	540	625	34
CANTERBURY	...	...	...	30	13	2	0	695	471	2	0	13	529	634	32
CREWE	...		...	30	14	0	1	754	377	1	0	14	503	662	30
EASTBOURNE	...	...	...	30	13	0	2	651½	505½	1	2	12	483	680	30
MIDDLESBROUGH	...	...	...	30	10	1	4	661	509	4	0	11	493	674	29
LONG EATON	...	...	...	30	11	0	4	622	539	3	1	11	475½	651½	29
IPSWICH	...	...	...	30	12	0	3	625	539	1	1	13	491	672	27
DONCASTER	...	...	...	30	9	0	6	602	558	3	0	12	463	700	24
NELSON	...	...	...	30	10	2	3	604½	560½	1	0	14	459	704	24
BERWICK	...	...	...	30	10	0	5	630½	528½	1	1	13	484½	676½	23
PLYMOUTH	...	...	...	30	9	0	6	629	534	0	0	15	371	783	18
KINGS LYNN II	...	...	...	30	6	1	8	576	582	2	0	13	449	708	17

BRITISH LEAGUE DIVISION ONE 1970

BELLE VUE	...	...	...	36	18	0	0	882½	517½	9	2	7	713	688	56
WIMBLEDON	...	...	...	36	18	0	0	859	541	4	2	12	647	756	46
COVENTRY	...	...	...	36	17	1	0	880	521	5	0	13	637½	766½	46
LEICESTER	...	...	...	36	16	0	2	771	631	5	0	13	652	750	42
POOLE	...	...	...	36	16	0	2	785	615	4	0	14	607	794	40
HALIFAX	...	...	...	36	17	0	1	855½	547½	2	1	15	637	767	39
SHEFFIELD	...	...	...	36	14	2	2	797½	606½	4	1	13	617	785	39
GLASGOW	...	...	...	36	17	1	0	832	570	1	0	17	606	797	37
WOLVERHAMPTON	...	...	...	36	15	1	2	791	612	1	1	16	580	821	34
EXETER	...	...	...	36	16	1	1	821	583	0	0	18	548½	851½	33
HACKNEY WICK	...	...	...	36	15	1	2	778	625	0	1	17	591½	810½	32
KINGS LYNN	...	...	...	36	14	0	4	774	629	2	0	16	585	814	32
OXFORD	...	...	...	36	14	0	4	772½	631½	2	0	16	588	814	32
WEMBLEY	...	...	...	36	13	2	3	738	665	2	0	16	589½	809½	32

CRADLEY HEATH	36	12	0	6	746½	648½	3	1	14	605	797	31
SWINDON	36	13	1	4	778	623	1	1	16	608	795	30
NEWCASTLE	36	15	0	3	794	610	0	0	18	570	834	30
WEST HAM	36	13	1	4	773	629	1	1	16	568½	834½	30
NEWPORT	36	10	0	8	718	685	2	0	16	540	863	24

BRITISH LEAGUE DIVISON TWO 1970

CANTERBURY	32	16	0	0	774	472	7	1	8	610	636	47
EASTBOURNE	32	16	0	0	788	458	6	1	9	576½	667½	45
ROCHDALE	32	16	0	0	842	395	5	2	9	618	625	44
BRADFORD	32	16	0	0	826	418	2	1	13	529	716	37
TEES-SIDE	32	15	0	1	752	492	3	0	13	552	694	36
IPSWICH...	32	13	2	1	717	529	4	0	12	537	707	36
CREWE	32	16	0	0	800	445	1	1	14	505	741	35
ROMFORD	32	12	0	4	702½	541½	5	1	10	551	690	35
READING	32	14	0	2	723	521	3	0	13	555½	690½	34
PETERBOROUGH ...	32	13	1	2	681	567	1	1	14	510	734	30
WORKINGTON ...	32	12	0	4	690	555	1	1	14	555	581	27
RAYLEIGH	32	12	1	3	666	577	1	0	15	489½	752½	27
BOSTON	32	10	1	5	658½	585½	2	1	13	485½	756½	26
CRAYFORD	32	11	1	4	682	561	0	0	16	471	777	23
DONCASTER	32	8	1	7	621½	616½	3	0	13	502	745	23
BERWICK	32	10	0	6	661	584	0	0	16	428	816	20
LONG EATON	32	8	3	5	613½	631½	0	0	16	474	769	19

BRITISH LEAGUE DIVISION ONE 1971

BELLE VUE	36	17	0	1	879	519	8	1	9	704	798	51
LEICESTER	36	13	1	4	795	607	9	2	7	695	702	47
COVENTRY	36	17	0	1	860	543	6	0	12	635	767	46
SHEFFIELD	36	18	0	0	827½	576½	3	1	14	622½	780½	43
SWINDON	36	13	1	4	766	636	6	2	10	647	756	41
READING	36	15	2	1	810½	589½	3	2	13	627½	771½	40
HACKNEY WICK... ...	36	13	0	5	762	641	4	4	10	648	752	38
NEWPORT	36	17	0	1	793	611	2	0	16	597	805	38
WEMBLEY	36	14	1	3	810	594	3	2	13	623	778	37
WIMBLEDON	36	16	1	1	796½	604½	2	0	16	592½	810½	37
POOLE	36	14	1	3	802	600	3	1	14	602	799	36
WOLVERHAMPTON ...	36	13	1	4	757	639	4	0	14	625	773	35
KINGS LYNN ...	36	12	2	4	746½	654½	4	0	14	650	752	34
HALIFAX	36	16	1	1	803	600	0	1	17	571	830	34
EXETER	36	14	0	4	793	607	2	0	16	586	817	32
GLASGOW	36	14	1	3	804	599	1	0	17	599	802	31
OXFORD	36	12	0	6	740	658	0	1	17	523½	879½	25
CRADLEY HEATH	36	8	4	6	717	685	0	0	18	581	822	20
WEST HAM	36	9	1	8	708	696	0	0	18	528	875	19

BRITISH LEAGUE DIVISION TWO 1971

EASTBOURNE	32	15	0	1	800	438	7	3	6	594	649	47
BRADFORD	32	16	0	0	778	468	5	1	10	592	651	43
IPSWICH...	32	14	1	1	746	495	6	2	8	599	646	43
BOSTON	32	15	0	1	744	503	3	3	10	568	670	39
RAYLEIGH	32	12	2	2	688	555	6	0	10	589	654	38
HULL	32	12	2	2	703	542	4	0	12	589	657	34

118

Team				P												
CREWE	...	...	...	32	15	1	0	826	418	1	0	15	475	766	33
BERWICK	...	...	...	32	16	0	0	784½	461½	0	0	16	500	747	32
ROCHDALE	...	...	...	32	14	0	2	700	544	2	0	14	477	767	32
LONG EATON	...	...	...	32	13	2	1	690	555	0	1	15	505	735	29
BIRMINGHAM	...	...	...	32	13	1	2	704	541	0	2	14	477	771	29
ROMFORD	...	...	...	32	12	0	4	700	542	1	0	15	522½	721½	26
TEES-SIDE	...	...	...	32	12	0	4	707½	536½	1	0	15	483½	762½	26
CANTERBURY	...	...	...	32	12	2	2	702	543	0	0	16	458	789	26
WORKINGTON	...	...	...	32	11	0	5	701	547	1	1	14	533	703	25
PETERBOROUGH	...	...	...	32	11	1	4	691	553	0	0	16	482	764	23
SUNDERLAND	...	...	...	32	9	1	6	635	600	0	0	16	398	847	19

BRITISH LEAGUE DIVISION ONE 1972

Team				P												
BELLE VUE	...	...	...	34	17	0	0	873½	449½	14	1	2	719	602	63
READING	...	...	...	34	17	0	0	806	518	10	1	8	648	676	51
KINGS LYNN	...	...	...	34	16	0	1	769	556	8	3	6	663	663	51
SHEFFIELD	...	...	...	34	13	1	3	804	521	10	2	5	684	642	49
LEICESTER	...	...	...	34	14	1	2	748	578	3	4	10	617	709	39
IPSWICH	...	...	...	34	11	1	5	728	594	6	0	11	604	719	35
POOLE	...	...	...	34	13	1	3	746	579	2	1	14	561	763	32
HACKNEY WICK	...	...	...	34	14	0	3	754	569	2	0	15	552	772	32
WOLVERHAMPTON	...	...	...	34	14	0	3	729	595	2	0	15	573	753	32
COVENTRY	...	...	...	34	12	2	3	756	568	2	0	15	571	749	30
EXETER	...	...	...	34	12	1	4	735½	590½	1	1	15	556	767	28
HALIFAX	...	...	...	34	12	2	3	713	612	1	0	16	548	776	28
WIMBLEDON	...	...	...	34	14	0	3	724	597	0	0	17	501	824	28
GLASGOW	...	...	...	34	11	2	4	730	595	1	0	16	533	790	26
SWINDON	...	...	...	34	12	1	4	736	589	0	0	17	578	748	25
CRADLEY HEATH	...	...	...	34	10	2	5	679	646	1	1	15	555½	770½	25
OXFORD	...	...	...	34	10	0	7	697	625	0	0	17	503½	818½	20
NEWPORT	...	...	...	34	9	0	8	658	666	0	0	17	481	844	18

BRITISH LEAGUE DIVISION TWO 1972

Team				P												
CREWE	...	...	...	32	15	0	1	834	413	7	1	8	610	628	45
BOSTON	...	...	...	32	16	0	0	785	461	5	1	10	580	666	43
PETERBOROUGH	...	...	...	32	14	0	2	738	508	7	0	9	574	671	42
RAYLEIGH	...	...	...	32	15	1	0	771	474	2	3	11	562	686	38
EASTBOURNE	...	...	...	32	15	1	0	771	469	3	1	12	552½	591½	38
BIRMINGHAM	...	...	...	32	15	1	0	782	462	3	0	13	547	695	37
WORKINGTON	...	...	...	32	15	0	1	777	468	3	0	13	531	715	36
HULL	...	...	...	32	12	0	4	673	574	4	0	12	550	695	32
BARROW	...	...	...	32	13	0	3	712	532	2	1	13	548	698	31
TEES-SIDE	...	...	...	32	14	1	1	728	516	0	2	14	490	754	31
BRADFORD	...	...	...	32	13	0	3	710	530	2	0	14	517	729	30
SUNDERLAND	...	...	...	32	13	1	2	702	541	0	1	15	478	765	28
CANTERBURY	...	...	...	32	11	0	5	717	526	2	1	13	512	724	27
BERWICK	...	...	...	32	11	3	2	671	575	1	0	15	485	755	27
ELLESMERE PORT	...	...	...	32	11	0	5	667	575	1	0	15	489	754	24
LONG EATON	...	...	...	32	10	2	4	655	589	1	0	15	449	796	24
SCUNTHORPE	...	...	...	32	5	1	10	580½	633½	0	0	16	402	841	11

CHEERS!

Some of the fruits of success

*Left: 'Cheers'—from Ivan
Mauger and actress Alexandra
Bastedo*

Below: Eric Boocock and Ivan swimming in cash!